Praise for *Following Jesus*

"The great challenge of being a Christian, I have found, is not just to believe in Jesus, or to admire Jesus, but to follow him. Using the interpretive lens of prophet, priest, and king, Tim Gaines, Kara Lyons-Pardue, and friends help us to see Jesus in fresh, life-giving ways. There are surprises and insights in every chapter that offer encouragement and practical help for those of us attempting to keep up with Jesus."

Will Willimon
Professor of the Practice of Christian Ministry, Duke Divinity School
Retired Bishop, United Methodist Church
Author, *Who Lynched Willie Earle? Preaching to Confront Racism*

"Anytime you mention the name of Jesus, things happen. It is a powerful name that brings peace, agitation, order, and messiness. Your instinct is to tame that name and put it in a box you can control and understand. But Gaines and Lyons-Pardue make clear that the tidy boxes we construct are really only imposing our own expectations on the One who is above all descriptors. Through the many people they have brought together, we are lifted above our own limitations to see that following Jesus is an exhilarating journey of unexpected discovery."

Kevin Mannoia
Chaplain, Azusa Pacific University
Former Bishop, Free Methodist Church
Former President, National Association of Evangelicals

"This engaging volume invites us to confront our assumptions about Jesus and allow them to be reshaped by the particularity of the Jesus of the Gospels. Each chapter probes the context and significance of Jesus's various roles as prophet, priest, or king and considers the profound implications for those who follow him. The authors' focus on how Jesus embodied justice, inclusion, advocacy, and reconciliation in Scripture—and on what this can look like in everyday life—is a particularly welcome addition. This book helps us move beyond abstraction and trite summaries, guiding us to develop Christ-shaped imaginations and to live into the hope of a new reality that Jesus as prophet, priest, and king has initiated."

Amy Brown Hughes
Assistant Professor of Theology
Gordon College

"*Following Jesus* provides a critical, thoughtful, and helpful examination of the implications of assigning the titles of prophet, priest, and king to Jesus. This book not only sheds light on Jesus's identity but also invites us to emulate him to shape our Christian identity and witness."

Abson P. Joseph
Academic Dean, Professor of New Testament
Wesley Seminary at Indiana Wesleyan University

D0234937

"At the heart of the gospel has always been the call to follow Jesus. This invitation is profoundly uncomplicated yet overwhelmingly complex. Like holding up a spectacular diamond for us to marvel at, the authors of *Following Jesus* introduce readers at every stage in the life of discipleship to the simple beauty of following Jesus while carefully articulating and marveling at the many beautiful and rich facets of discipleship."

Scott Daniels
Lead Pastor, Nampa College Church of the Nazarene
Nampa, ID

"Taking the time to remove the things that may be blinding us to a clear vision of Jesus is necessary if we want to be his faithful followers. In *Following Jesus*, Lyons-Pardue and Gaines have gathered together an outstanding team of writers who will take you on a challenging journey, bringing clarity to understanding Jesus as prophet, priest, and king. Whether a minister, student, or layperson, this book will be an invaluable resource for the serious follower of Jesus Christ."

Carla Sunberg
General Superintendent
Church of the Nazarene

FOLLOWING

JESUS

FOLLOWING
JESUS

Prophet, Priest, King

Timothy R. Gaines *and*
Kara Lyons-Pardue, *Editors*

THE FOUNDRY
PUBLISHING

Copyright © 2018 by Beacon Hill Press of Kansas City
Beacon Hill Press of Kansas City
PO Box 419527
Kansas City, MO 64141
beaconhillbooks.com

978-0-8341-3687-8

Printed in the
United States of America

Cover Design: J.R. Caines
Interior Design: Sharon Page

Library of Congress Cataloging-in-Publication Data
Names: Gaines, Timothy R., 1981- editor.
Title: Following Jesus : prophet, priest, king / Timothy R. Gaines and Kara   Lyons-Pardue, editors.
Description: Kansas City, MO : Beacon Hill Press of Kansas City, 2018. | Includes bibliographical references.
Identifiers: LCCN 2017058155 (print) | LCCN 2017061254 (ebook) | ISBN 9780834136885 (ebook) |
    ISBN 9780834136878 (pbk.)
Subjects: LCSH: Jesus Christ—Person and offices—Biblical teaching. | Jesus Christ—Example—Biblical teaching.
Classification: LCC BT250 (ebook) | LCC BT250 .F65 2018 (print) | DDC 232/.8—dc23
LC record available at https://lccn.loc.gov/2017058155.

The internet addresses, email addresses, and phone numbers in this book are accurate at the time of publication. They are provided as a resource. Beacon Hill Press of Kansas City does not endorse them or vouch for their content or permanence.

10 9 8 7 6 5 4 3 2 1

From Kara
For my children, Zoe and Iris. May you know, love,
and follow Jesus all your days.

From Tim
For the people of Southeast and BFC. Thank you for following Jesus well.

✝ CONTENTS

✝ INTRODUCTION

Kara Lyons-Pardue

FOR MORE than two millennia, followers of Jesus have sought to know everything we can know about our Savior. And, for that same amount of time, we have had to admit that our answers are incomplete. No title for or explanation of Jesus fully encapsulates who Jesus was and is.

Recently, I was asked how motherhood is going, which is a perfectly valid question. Yet it is also a question that could render five hundred very different but equally true responses, none of which would be comprehensive. Being a mother is joyous. It is also tiring. Parenting my two daughters exposes my impatience. Yet a mere smile from my baby can immediately brighten my day, and my four-year-old's sense of humor keeps me in stitches. My role as mother can keep me awake at night, plagued by worries. At the same time, no other responsibility has taught me as much about trusting God as this one. Most of us understand, instinctively, the complexity of human relationships like parent, spouse, friend, and child. Nevertheless, we seem to want our descriptions of Jesus to fit neatly in a fully understood box. Even our most elaborate creeds, approved by church councils long ago, cannot explicate Jesus's identity fully.

When he wrote at the end of the second century, the early church father Irenaeus described the four stories about Jesus (our four Gospels), and their relationship to Jesus himself, with a biblical metaphor. He said that the four Gospels are like the creatures surrounding the heavenly throne in Ezekiel's and the Revelator's visions (Ezek. 1:5–14; Rev. 4:6–8), providing an image of how the Gospels function that has stuck across the centuries.[1] These fantastic

---

1. Irenaeus, *Against Heresies* III.11.8.

creatures that are like a lion, ox, eagle, and man *are not* God, even as they point in holy reverence *to* the divine presence. The Gospels, likewise, point to Jesus, even as they cannot contain him. It is not that the Son is many divergent things—to some a lion, to some an eagle; to some a friend, to others a prophet—he is one divine person. Yet our encounters with Jesus are, by definition, incomplete and limited because of *our* limitations.

Almost as ancient as Irenaeus, Eusebius tried to hold onto this multifaceted vision of Jesus while giving us familiar titles that could point us to Jesus's complex identity. He described Christ's "threefold office" as prophet, priest, and king, as anticipated and supported by Old Testament Scripture.[2] Eusebius sought to protect Christianity—and its Christ—from accusations of being an upstart religion: the date of Jesus's incarnation ought not distract us from his true antiquity and divinity. Today, however, the inverse is more often the temptation: Jesus is taken to be divine—eclipsing prophet, priest, and king—without giving much thought to the realities of his incarnation. This book seeks to linger in the tension of Jesus's particular identity and incarnate roles once again.

The three titles prophet, priest, and king have some glaring problems at first glance, some of which Eusebius himself acknowledged.[3] When Jesus was called a prophet during his ministry, his responses indicate that that title was not entirely incorrect but was, perhaps, inadequate (Mark 8:27–30; John 4:16–26). Further, we have no indication that anyone ever called Jesus a priest during his earthly ministry—probably because, as a descendant of Judah, he was automatically disqualified from priesthood, a role reserved for descendants of the tribe of Levi (Num. 18). In fact, he does not seem to have engaged with other priests much during his ministry as the Gospels depict it (cf. Matt. 8:4/Mark 1:44/Luke 5:14). When he finally has face time with the Jerusalem priesthood, it does not end well for him (e.g., Matt. 26:57–68). The final problem is that no one called Jesus a king except for those who wished to mock him at his crucifixion. The closest we get to an attribution of kingship to Jesus is from a select few—including Peter (Luke 9:20), the Samaritan woman (John 4:29), and Martha (John 11:27)—who refer to his anointed status (i.e., Messiah/Christ). As David Young indicates in chapter 9, this anointed status—which has kingly echoes—is part of what

---

2. *Church History* I.3.8.

3. Eusebius mentions this difficulty of ancestry outright in *Church History* I.3.11, 17–18.

we are confessing when we say "Christ." Yet, when Peter confessed Jesus as Messiah, he and the other disciples were roundly shushed (Mark 8:30; Luke 9:21). Only after Jesus's resurrection do we find Christians openly declaring that Jesus is Messiah. Then, in relatively short order, his title "Christ" (*Christos*, Greek for "Messiah") becomes so frequent that we often wrongly treat it as Jesus's last name.[4]

Even as we acknowledge the limitations and odd fit of these three titles, they have stuck in Christian confession because they point us to true aspects of Jesus's life, ministry, and nature. These three titles have stuck, and so have stuck our assumptions about each role. Surely a prophet's main job is to tell the future, right? A priest is supposed to remain separate and holy, perhaps even celibate—isn't he? A king comes in frightening power when he reigns, we imagine. Each of these assumptions may offer a glimmer of truth, but they miss the point. When we apply these roles to Jesus, they are radically redefined and reshaped. Jesus is the one who sets the bar as prophet, priest, and king. This book, then, seeks to investigate who Jesus is in each role and what implications for us these parts of Jesus's identity have for following him.

Timothy R. Gaines, in chapter 1 on particularity, makes a compelling case for the need to examine and interrogate our assumptions about Jesus. It sometimes turns out that the generalized Jesus of our imagination is a poor fit with the real, particular Jesus we encounter in Scripture. I urge readers to sit with the profound implications of Jesus's incarnation: that Jesus actually lived—in an actual time, in an actual place, surrounded by actual people. The impact of this reality is not merely retroactive (i.e., changing how we think about Jesus in the past). As Gaines insists, it makes a difference in our actual lives today. This chapter sets the theological tone for the book as a whole. Each author has endeavored to take seriously the specifics of our witnesses to Jesus, challenging generalizations and platitudes when necessary.

Timothy Green introduces the Old Testament prophetic tradition and how Jesus fits the role of prophet (and how he does not) in chapter 2. As a long-time Old Testament professor, Green's presentation of the prophetic

---

4. For a mere fraction of the available examples, see: Acts 2:38; 3:6; Rom. 1:4; 1 Cor. 1:2; 2 Cor. 1:2–3; Gal. 2:16; Eph. 5:20; Phil. 1:11; 4:23; Col. 1:3; 1 Thess. 1:1; 2 Thess. 2:1; 1 Tim. 6:14; 2 Tim. 2:8; Titus 1:1; Phlm. 3; Heb. 10:10; James 1:1; 1 Pet. 1:1–3; 2 Pet. 1:16; 1 John 2:1; Jude 25; Rev. 1:1.

message draws on a deep familiarity with the wider body of Hebrew prophetic literature. He notes common trajectories of the prophetic message in the face of unfaithfulness and, conversely, faithfulness through hardship. In continuity, Jesus's willingness to speak uncomfortable truths to those in seats of power and to advocate on the part of the downtrodden fits both established prophetic trajectories. Green notes Jesus's consistency in light of God's faithful prophets of old, as well as his uniqueness. Unlike prophets before (and after) him, Jesus did not only speak as a mouthpiece for the divine message; rather, he *was* the incarnate Word of God among us.

The book's most interactive chapter is chapter 3, in which Stephanie Smith Matthews does not merely write *about* Jesus and the prophetic imagination but also guides readers to engage in cultivating a sensitivity to the prophetic imagination. She draws from three exemplary prophetic figures—Zechariah, Jesus, and Martin Luther King, Jr.—in whom she locates patterns of faithfulness that Christians today can emulate. The chapter provides focused reflection prompts, prayer guides, and gracious explanations toward the practices of introspection into sensitive areas. The rights and privileges to which we cling most tightly are often those the Spirit of God is challenging us, through the prophets, to release. In Matthews's chapter, the hope of this book—that understanding Jesus better might lead us into new avenues of following Jesus—is put into practice.

In chapter 4, written by me, Kara Lyons-Pardue, Jesus's treatment of women—from disciples, to encounters in his ministry, to his teaching—is in focus. The chapter draws out the prophetic implications of these interactions. If we understand Jesus's engagement with women to be embodying the intentions of God for relationships in the kingdom, then these gospel stories function as a prophetic glimpse of the world made right. What we notice, again and again, is a wholehearted welcome of women from myriad backgrounds. Jesus hears, teaches, and restores women. This chapter's final section examines and provides suggestions for how Jesus's prophetic welcome of women should instruct Christian men and women's practices and dispositions today.

In her chapter on Jesus as priest, chapter 5, Amy Peeler highlights the limited but rich passages of Scripture in which Jesus's priestly identity is evident. She leads the reader through John 17 and a thorough sweep of the book of Hebrews. This latter text is Peeler's specialty, which becomes evident as she connects sections and disparate themes to demonstrate the complex argumentation of the book. This argumentation, of course, exists to illustrate the utter supremacy of Jesus to all others, including the entire sacrificial system and priesthood. Carefully, though, Peeler illustrates that Hebrews does not undertake a slash-and-burn campaign on this sacred religious institution but, instead, operates christologically. The temple system's insufficiency is only in light of the utter and exceeding sufficiency for salvation of the great divine-human Mediator, Jesus Christ.

Diane Leclerc's chapter 6 represents a deep passion of hers and a message the church needs to heed. Leclerc investigates what the crucifixion means for salvation for Jesus's followers. After introducing the key issues in atonement theories—particularly in terms of how they relate to Jesus our great High Priest, both God and human—she moves beyond the conventional questions of how sinners experience salvation. Although those are crucial questions, Leclerc focuses on a neglected area of atonement theology: how the cross may symbolize salvation for those who are sinned-against, victimized, or abused. Her poignant chapter takes seriously Christ's own suffering, in all its ugliness, and points us toward God's appeal to the victimized.

Dick O. Eugenio engages Jesus's way of reconciliation in chapter 7. The term "mediation" is the one Wesley used to discuss reconciliation, with Christ as the mediator between humanity and God in his priestly role. Eugenio's interweaving of theological topics deftly connects Jesus's incarnation (becoming one of us) with his atonement—using the imagery of his sacrifice on our behalf—and his intercession and advocacy on our behalf. Jesus's ongoing work of reconciliation for us models the priesthood of reconciliation to which believers are called. This calling, Eugenio insists, is not one to be undertaken alone but in community. In one of his concluding lines, he states, "Only when Christlike generosity, kindness, and loving inclusiveness characterize our Christian communities can we expect others to believe in the biblical message of reconciliation."

In chapter 8, Gift Mtukwa spends time in Hebrews' descriptions of holiness, emphasizing how we learn from and access holiness through Jesus. The description is upbeat and hopeful. Jesus's unique priesthood has direct implications for our own sharing in his holiness. He shares a brief application of holiness within his African context, which offers a unique perspective on the distinctive call of Jesus's holiness that surely can be applied to other cultural contexts. Our holiness will not be explained simply, just as Jesus's cannot be.

Mtukwa's chapter resonates in harmony with the ancient statement of the early church that Christ became what we are *so that we might become as he is*. Pastors and teachers in Wesleyan-Holiness denominational traditions often speak of holiness as a "distinctive" of our branch in the Christian family, but, as Mtukwa argues, holiness cannot be owned by one group but, rather, should distinguish all Christians who follow the holy Christ.

David Young, in chapter 9 on Jesus as king, highlights how Jesus's identity as Messiah carries with it kingly implications. Young drives home the crucial point, however, that our expectations of kings do not define who Jesus is. Instead, Jesus's life redefines how we are to understand true kingship. Reading through several passages in Mark 8, Young highlights the extent of Jesus's manifest kingship and its redefinition of our expectations. Jesus's own followers needed their expectations to be altered profoundly in order to see Jesus for the king he was, just as we need to reimagine how we relate to power in light of Christ today.

In chapter 10 Mary K. Schmitt outlines four implications of the way on which Jesus leads us, again focusing on Mark's Gospel, which calls for a radical rejection of many of Jesus's society's (and our society's) most sacred and accepted values. Led by Mark, Schmitt draws out practical dispositions that reflect those Jesus modeled: holding loosely to possessions, restoration of community, accountability, and servant leadership. She also notes that this king's particular way led to a coronation, that looked to all the world like mockery and scorn. Schmitt's chapter also briefly illustrates the theological kinship between Mark's and John's Gospels: where John makes clear in his talk about crucifixion as being "lifted up" (an actual and ironic, cruciform enthronement; see John 12:32; 17:1–5), Mark only hints.

Scripture does not give us an easy answer regarding how following King Jesus orients us to the competing kings and rulers in our world today, as Timothy L. P. Hahn explains in chapter 11. He does, however, offer plenty of guidance regarding the proper Christian orientation of worship. Hahn provides three models that Christians have used historically in relating Jesus to our Caesars, explaining the benefits and costs of each. Ultimately, Hahn does not find any of the three models perfectly satisfying. However we approach the tension between living under the lordship of Christ while also living under the government of other rulers, Hahn suggests the characteristics of a "Christomorphic imagination" that can guide us faithfully.

In chapter 12, Ryan L. Hansen traces the call to worship and the character of the slain Lamb, who is worthy of worship, in the book of Revelation. This call, as Hansen makes clear, is at once theological and political (both in its ancient context and as we read it today). Hymns of praise punctuate Revelation, providing direction and theological clarity amid the vivid imagery of the Revelator's visions. Hansen attends to the complex considerations of the apocalyptic genre and its characteristic symbolism. In the midst of careful exegesis, Hansen notes the beautiful optimism of praise conveyed in the hymns that sing of the end of Caesar's reign and the beginning of the Lamb's rule. It is fitting that this compilation on *Following Jesus* should conclude with such costly but optimistic hope as we follow this slain Lamb into renewed life.

Throughout the book, we make use of explanatory footnotes that represent an effort to educate and provide background for readers who need it. For example, several of our authors refer to a specific period in Israel's history, the Maccabean (or Hasmonean) period. Because this period occurs between the timetables of the Old and New Testaments and is only referenced in detail in the Deuterocanonical (or Apocryphal) books, many Protestants are ignorant of this historical period shortly prior to Jesus's time. Yet this backdrop is crucial for understanding the expectations and hero stories in which Jesus and his contemporaries would have been steeped. Military and priestly leadership led Israel in holy rebellion to take back their land from foreign invaders with no respect for the righteousness of Israel's God. Their dynasty fizzled out with the Roman conquest of Palestine less than a century before Jesus's birth (63 BCE).

Yet this era of Israelite independence loomed large in the minds of Jesus's contemporaries. As evidence that we might not otherwise notice, a high percentage of the names of Jesus's friends and disciples (male and female) recorded in the New Testament are names prominent in the Maccabean (Hasmonean) royal lineage.[5] This family of warrior-priest-kings inaugurated

---

5. Judas (not Iscariot), for instance, was the most famous Maccabean brother (see 1 Macc. 3:1–2), the one whose nickname gave the movement its name (*maqqabi*/Maccabee = hammer; see Isa. 44:12). Several of Jesus's followers, and one of his brothers, were named Judas (sometimes abbreviated to Jude in English). Mary, the name of approximately one-quarter of women in Palestine in the centuries surrounding Jesus's life, took several forms in Greek—Maria, Mariam, Mariamme—all of which recalled Moses's sister, Miriam, and was also the name of many Maccabean royal women. See Tal Ilan, *Lexicon of Jewish*

ancient Israel's last war for independence—and won. In that light, how could this history *not* impact the perspectives of those around Jesus?

Beyond the footnotes, for readers interested in these stories, the Apocryphal books of 1 and 2 Maccabees are widely available online or in any print Bible containing the Old Testament Deuterocanonical books (i.e., the Apocrypha). These are Jewish accounts written during the intertestamental period (that is, between the Old and New Testaments), which were read by both Jews and Christians. Just like us, Jesus's contemporaries had a preexisting set of stories and allegiances that informed their encounters with Jesus. It is good for us to be aware of their contexts and biases just as we should attempt to name our own.

The theological affirmations of Scripture are not separable from their historical context, like a kernel from its husk (unlike what Adolf von Harnack famously claimed). Instead, the reality of Jesus's incarnation—that is, that the Son, truly God, was born and grew and became a man, truly human—ties together forever the course of human history and the reality of God. The further implication of this confession that taking history seriously is vital for understanding Jesus is that our context matters too. Where we are in space, time, and culture must necessarily shape our understanding of Jesus. This is not an imposition on or a lessening of Jesus's identity; it is a necessary corollary of us taking Jesus as real, living, and reigning and *not* as an abstraction.

Throughout these chapters, we seek to take ancient and modern history seriously. And we endeavor to apply an ancient testimony about *who* Jesus is to us—our ultimate Prophet, Priest, and King—in ways that hit home in our world today. If you begin to feel uncomfortable as you read one of these chapters, we encourage you to prayerfully discern, carefully consider, and openly discuss within your church community what might be causing the discomfort. The Spirit can prick our consciences to help us discern when we are encountering error or misapplying some truth, certainly. But it is even more uncomfortable to be confronted with an idol we have set up in place of the living Christ. It hurts to lay down the assumptions we have created or inherited that protect us from confronting the demands of a holy

---

Names in Late Antiquity: Part I, Palestine 330 BCE–200 CE (Tübingen, Germany: Mohr Siebeck, 2002), 242–44. Jesus's own mother and many of his women followers were named Mary, as the Gospels attest.

Jesus who wishes to be Lord of our lives. May we encounter the crucified and resurrected Jesus so that we may follow him more fully.

1 ✝ FOLLOWING JESUS: THE PATH OF PARTICULARITY

Timothy R. Gaines

"JESUS will just knock your socks off!" she exclaimed as she handed me her phone. The screen on her device displayed a series of pictures of a sunglasses-wearing couple seated in a red convertible and surrounded by palm trees. "See these people? Jesus sent them on vacation! They started praying, and now they spend a month in the islands every year. Jesus is just blowing them away!"

Our conversation was my first with this woman, whom I had met that afternoon. It didn't take long before our polite chitchat turned to matters of faith and, eventually, to Jesus. As I reflected on our conversation, I wondered about the way she spoke of Jesus. Was Jesus really the one sending her friends on tropical vacations? The Jesus I read about in the Gospel accounts, for example, was the one constantly calling his followers to lay down their lives and pick up their crosses. Nowhere in the Gospels could I remember reading about the vacation package Jesus offered his follow-ers. Of course, I also couldn't remember anywhere in the Gospel accounts where Jesus declared vacations to be outright evil, but the conversation got me wondering about the kinds of ideas we have in mind about Jesus, where we get those ideas, and how those ideas measure up to the actual things Jesus said and did. To use the word at the center of this chapter's theme, it got me wondering about how much the *particularity* of Jesus matters for those seeking to follow him.

Particularity is a technical-sounding word, but at its heart, it simply points to the reality that, when we are talking about Jesus, we are talking about a real-life, human person who offers his followers a very particular way to follow.[1] In other words, his in-the-flesh existence resists our efforts to make him into something he is not because, as a particular person, he did and said certain things, and those things must inform the way we follow him. Just like every other human to have ever lived, Jesus's life took on a specific shape. Just like you and me, he did particular things, and he said particular things. Just like you and me, Jesus was not generically human but, rather, became human in a very specific way, and that specific way is loaded with meaning for the way we understand Jesus as a prophet, a priest, and a king.

Perhaps my conversation partner would have objected to the kind of thing I'm discussing here by saying something like, "But Jesus was blessing my friends! Doesn't Jesus want us to be blessed?" I think the obvious response here is yes, but this is the pesky thing about Jesus's particularity: the kind of blessing he offers doesn't always match our definition of that word. "Blessed are you," Jesus tells us, "when people insult you, persecute you and say all kinds of evil against you because of me" (Matt. 5:11). When Jesus enters Jerusalem as king, he does so in a very particular way, redrawing kingship in his image and inviting us to align ourselves with the kind of kingdom led by a king on a donkey, rather than a king on a warhorse (Matt. 21:1–11; Mark 11:1–11; Luke 19:28–44; John 12:12–19).

In the same way, Jesus is no enemy of family, but he drastically redefines the concept of family in an awfully particular way, opting for and adopting those who have given themselves to God, rather than favoring his blood relations (Matt. 12:46–50). Or consider the way Jesus uses power throughout his life. Knowing that the Father has placed all power into his hands, Jesus immediately uses those hands not to promote himself but to take up the very particular task of washing his disciples' feet (John 13:3–5). The book of Revelation presents a vividly particular image of Jesus's way of occupying the place of kingly glory in the new creation: where we would expect to see a roaring lion we instead, shockingly, behold a lamb "that looked as if it had been slaughtered" (Rev. 5:6, NLT).

In just about any way we can try to fit him into our expectations, Jesus's particularity redemptively shatters those expectations, resetting our imaginations and directing our feet to holy paths we could not walk alone. Jesus's

---

1. The word "particularity" has its origins in Latin and shares a common root with "particle," signaling a meaning having to do with being distinct.

"particular way leaves no sphere of life untouched as he goes about his work of bringing a new, eternal way of life into the midst of the old. The old ways, though, are so familiar and comfortable to us that Jesus's call to walk in his new way often presents us with challenges we would rather ignore, especially if the old way has been effective at lulling us into comfort. It is Jesus, human in a very particular way, who reveals to his followers what God looks like, and what it looks like to be a true prophet, a faithful priest, and a good king.

If all of this feels a tad fuzzy, maybe this story will be helpful. When I was a high school student, I lived in a small town at the base of a mountain range. Each fall, our school's football team played a rival school, located in the mountains east of our town. The morning before these games, the student body assembled for a pep rally, which unfortunately included a series of chants, cheers, and activities designed to encourage our team at the expense of our opponents' reputation. In the name of rallying the team to impending victory, we were told that they were "mountain folk," unsophisticated, primitive, and unrefined Neanderthals with questionable genetic lineage. I wish I were making this up. The point, of course, was to create in the minds of my classmates a negative idea of what it was like to be a student at our rival school, and it seemed to work. When we arrived at the stadium that evening, we also came with the expectation that the opposing team's players all fell into the same category of crude brute. We had the same, generalized idea about them all.

Several weeks after one of these games one year, I traveled to the town where our rival school was located, where I encountered a young man about my age in a bookstore who attended the rival school. As it turned out, he loved art and music and was well read and knowledgeable about literature. He was a well-spoken, interesting conversation partner. He was, in fact, nothing like the *idea* I had come to expect about who he was. At that point, I had a choice. I could either reject the notion that he was actually from our rival school —because he didn't fit my expectations—or, I could be compelled to reform my ideas and expectations based upon the *particularity* of the person standing in front of me.

The incarnation of Jesus functions in a similar way. Many of us have been given ideas about who Jesus is and how he should act. We may have ideas about how we want him to act on our behalf as a prophet, a priest, and/or a king. We might even try to make him fit the ideas we have in mind about him. But when we encounter him in his particularity, our choices are similar to the ones I had that day in the bookstore: we must either make him fit our ideas, or we must allow his unique particularity to reshape our ideas. One of the unique aspects of Christian faith, then, is not that our understanding of God is derived from our *ideas* about what a divine being should be like and do but, rather, that our understanding of God comes from a living, in-the-flesh person who lived in a very particular way, revealing to us who God is and what God is like. If this is the way Christians come to understand God, then we will need to give special and careful attention to the witness of the Gospel accounts of the New Testament, allowing them to enliven our understanding of the person we follow as prophet, priest, and king.[2]

There has historically been a tension between prophets, priests, and kings, especially in Jesus's day, making it all the more interesting to consider him fulfilling all three roles. The priests of Israel, as we will see later, were mediators between a holy God and a people who were called to be holy. Among the group of priests, called Levites, that kind of mediation required a certain amount of withdrawal from the surrounding world because so much of the world could contaminate one's purity. Prophets were another distinct voice in Israel's history, often crying out to their people to remind them that being a holy people did not require withdrawal from but engagement of the people living at the margins of society. Care for the poor and disempowered was a hallmark of the prophets' vision of holiness, which presented a challenge to the kind of priestly retraction one might find among the Levites. Kingship—a role added later in Israel's history, yet significant nonetheless—functioned as the office of political governance. The record of

---

2. This is not always a simple act when we take into account that each of the Gospel writers highlights certain aspects of Jesus's life and ministry. The Gospel writers, while offering us a *faithful* account of Jesus's life, were not especially interested in giving to us a completely *unified* account. Though this might seem to present serious challenges to the possibility of taking account of Jesus's particularity, we should remember that the Gospel writers are giving us an account of a living person whose particularity cannot be contained in the pages of their accounts. In other words, even though the Gospels may not convey every detail of Jesus's life, they do give us a picture of a distinct person who invites us to walk in his particular way. Each of the Gospel accounts offers us a different side of the picture; their differences point to the living complexity of a person whose particularity cannot be contained in a written document.

kings in Israel's history is spotty; there were just as many scoundrels on the throne as there were heroes of faithfulness. Perhaps we don't expect kings to be as holy as priests or as motivated toward justice as prophets. But Jesus wraps up all three roles in his particularity, gathering them into his fleshly, on-the-ground comings, goings, preachings, and healings. Doing this as a flesh-and-blood person, Jesus holds together the roles of prophet, priest, and king so that each role not only rubs off on the other, but all three together are defined according to the particularity of his life and ministry.

Naming Jesus according to all three titles, then, is a fascinating move because his particularity comes to re-narrate and redefine all three roles. He mediates the holiness of God not by withdrawal from anything or anyone unclean but by prophetic engagement with the least of these. His prophetic call is a call to holiness, but any justice he achieves is always a result of contact with God's holiness. His kingship is just as prophetic as it is priestly because his governance guides us toward a holy justice. If we are looking for any of these roles to make sense out of Jesus, we've got it backward. Rather, the particularity of who he is exposes the shortcomings of prophets, priests, and kings—even while he graciously offers his own life as the alternative.

For thousands of years, Christians have been pondering, "*How* could the divine possibly become something that was not? In what way did Jesus become human *and* divine? Were there human parts and divine parts? What exactly took place? *How* has Jesus become God and human?" While questions like these are worthy of our time and investigation, I'd like to adjust our approach slightly by exclaiming, "Look at *who* God has become in flesh!" In other words, the questions driving this book are not so much concerned with the theological mechanics of *how* Jesus was both fully divine and fully human as they are concerned with *who* a fully God and fully human person is as a prophet, a priest, and a king.[3] When we talk about Jesus's particularity, we are not only talking about the breathtaking reality that God became flesh, but we are also saying that the *kind* of flesh Jesus became, and the *kinds* of things he did in the flesh, profoundly shape the way we follow him.

Looking at how Jesus demonstrates what it means to be a prophet, a priest, and a king will require us to take an account of the particularities

---

3. Dietrich Bonhoeffer's *Christ the Center* is helpful on this point.

of his life, death, resurrection, and ascension. Jesus doesn't simply slip into the predefined roles of prophet, priest, and king; rather, he becomes the living example of what these roles are and how they ought to function. We must make no mistake: Jesus will do this on his terms. When we talk about Jesus's particularity, we are talking about him setting the model for prophets, priests, and kings, rather than conforming himself to some other standard. Each chapter that follows will be an invitation to take further and fuller account of what it means to take Jesus's particularity seriously if we allow him to set the model for being a prophet, a priest, and a king. If he is setting the model, he is also shaping the way we follow him. He is a prophet in *this* way, a priest in *this* way, and a king in *this* way—and that has serious implications for those who follow him.

If we are honest, that truth is probably a bit unsettling, even as it is refreshingly redemptive. What king, for example, does the work of being a king like Jesus? What king cares so little about propping up the political power of his own people or making them into a bigger, stronger, richer, greater version of what they were before? What king calls his people to exist by giving themselves away, even as he gives himself away? What kind of kingdom can be led by a man who calls the kingdom to the way of loving others at the kingdom's own expense? This is either the most foolish political strategy to ever befall human history, or it is the politics of particularity—the particular way Jesus goes about being a king.

Acknowledging Jesus as fully human and fully divine means that he becomes for us not only what it looks like to be fully human but also what it looks like to be fully divine. If we take the particularity of Jesus seriously, all the concepts we have about God need to be measured by who he is in the flesh, what he does, how he acts, how he lives, and even how he dies. The particular things Jesus does and says cannot be overlooked when it comes to his revelation of God to us. What might it tell us about God that God not only became flesh but also became the flesh of a peasant? How might our understanding of God be shaped by the reality that God's in-the-flesh revelation was a laborer from the wrong side of the tracks? For those who confess that God became flesh, it matters that, in flesh, God unsettled really righteous folks who were deeply convinced of their own theology and religious practice. It matters that he opted for friends and followers whom the rest of society had overlooked and written off. It matters that he would engage unholy places with an uncommon holiness. It matters that he did not fit into any of the common political parties of his day. It matters that he had an affinity for outcasts and challenged insiders. It matters that he was far more interested in faithfulness than comfort. It matters because his particularity—the things he did and did not do, the things he said and did not say—stands before us, asking how far we would really be willing to go to follow Jesus if his particularity refuses to be usurped by what we wish him to be.

The particularity of Jesus often explodes upon our desires of what we wish him to be—the way he will be a prophet for us, a priest for us, and a king for us. It is a redemptive explosion, but it can be jarring, nonetheless. This was the case for those who encountered Jesus in the first century, and it remains the case for us today. Philosophers and theologians have observed of Western culture that the increasing presence of multiple religious traditions, civic commitments, economic realities, and approaches to spirituality offers a tantalizing possibility: to combine those influences into something that will easily fit and support our chosen lifestyle.[4] In a world of available consumer options, Jesus is an easy choice—as long as he helps us toward whatever goals we have in mind. In this approach, we still want to maintain the emotional benefits of belief in a transcendent God but without all the particular baggage that comes with it, such as specific religious practices, spiritual disciplines, and the like.

Late-modern Western civilization is beginning to opt for a mode of religious belief that dismisses the particularity of a peasant carpenter from Nazareth who called his followers to pick up a cross, deny themselves, and find salvation in doing so. We modern folk tend to be fine with adding Jesus into a lifestyle we've already cultivated, so long as his particularity doesn't mess with too many of our own choices. As long as we can smooth off the rough edges that cut against our chosen lifestyle, Jesus is fine, but if he begins to do the work of a prophet by calling us to turn away from our deeply held practices of unfaithfulness to God, he becomes problematically particular. If he does the work of a priest by mediating to us a God who doesn't fit our ideas of what God ought to be, his particularity begins to chafe. If he is the kind of king who goes so far as to challenge our politics, we can begin to understand how he ended up on a Roman cross after only a few years of public ministry.

---

4. See Charles Taylor, *A Secular Age* (Cambridge: Harvard University Press, 2007); and James K. A. Smith, *How (Not) to Be Secular* (Grand Rapids: Eerdmans, 2014).

A Jesus who is vague enough to fit easily into given hopes, conventions, and systems of life may be convenient—a kind of religious accessory to an upwardly mobile, middle-class lifestyle—but that is not the Jesus of the Gospels who confronts us, "full of grace and truth" (John 1:14). Herein is the mystery of the gospel: the good news of God comes to us in a very particular, challenging person named Jesus, who offers salvation by turning everything on its head. The hope of the gospel is not that we simply become more highly functioning participants in a lifestyle of our own choosing but that our lives become aligned with the particular way Jesus calls us to walk, however disruptive it may first appear.

We come now to this challenging reality about particularity: we can't make Jesus into whatever we wish him to be. His particularity means that we won't be able to enlist him in a project that isn't true to his particular way, nor can we make him fit any of our preconceptions of how a prophet, a priest, or a king is supposed to act. When God became flesh, it meant that God was going to encounter us in a very specific way, through very specific actions. Like any other person in the flesh, God's actions were concrete, embodied, physical actions. Jesus's incarnation refused to let him be nebulous or vague. As much as it may be at odds with our modern social sensibilities, we can't make Jesus into a person who left religious folks unchallenged, or one who neatly enfolded the political, civic, and religious aspects of life into one, easy-to-handle formula. His particularity shakes us—one of the reasons his particularity has often been called a scandal—and presents us with a new way of being a prophet, a priest, and a king.

Jesus is a particular *person*, and while this may land on us as one of the most baldly obvious statements of this book so far, it has profound implications for the way we believe in him as a prophet, a priest, and a king. As a prophet, he is doing more than delivering a set of truth propositions with which we might choose to agree. As a priest, he is doing more than packaging information about God and delivering it to us. As a king, he is doing more than propping up whatever our political preferences might be. In Jesus, God is filling out and redefining what it means to be a prophet, a priest, and a king—and doing it according to the particular life we see in Jesus.

Walking the Path of Particularity

How, then, might we follow Jesus with an eye toward his particularity? There are a number of ways his particularity offers us a redemptive challenge, but I'll outline just a few here.

First, following him in his particularity moves Christian faith away from being an ideology and instead makes it a way of life to be walked. Jesus's particularity challenges us to believe not only with our hearts and minds but also with our feet. If God had remained uninvolved in and distant from creation, it might make some amount of sense to believe in God by simply agreeing with ideas about who God is and what God does. But when God became flesh in the particular person of Jesus and Jesus began to call people to follow him, our belief became not only a matter of what we *think* about Jesus but also what we *do* to follow his way.[5]

Matthew, Mark, and Luke each give us an on-the-ground approach to the question of the way we believe in a God who became flesh. You can almost feel the breeze flowing off the waters of the Sea of Galilee in Matthew's account of Jesus encountering Peter and Andrew (4:18). "Come, follow me," Jesus requests of them, and that is precisely what they do (v. 19). Luke's account is more detailed, and even a touch more miraculous, as Jesus asks Peter to put the nets into the water, resulting in a catch capable of capsizing the boat (5:1–11). But at the end of it all, these fishermen "left everything and followed him" (v. 11). They believed not only with their minds but also with their feet.

We could have a bit of fun speculating about things that Matthew does not say in his account of Jesus calling the first disciples. Imagine the curious response Jesus might have received from Peter had he walked up to that group of fishermen with a list of statements about who Jesus was. "Do you agree with all of these statements about me?" Jesus might have asked, showing them a scroll that listed assertions such as, "Jesus is the Messiah. Jesus

---

5. In the ancient world around the time of Jesus, this would have been a relatively common understanding of belief. The philosophies of ancient Greek culture largely made belief about agreement with unseen ideas. According to the popular philosophy of the day, the universe was understood as being divided into two realms, the eternal and the temporal. As physical beings, we occupied the temporal realm, filled up with material substances like human bodies, dirt, water, air, and anything else that had a physical presence. The eternal realm, on the other hand, was where *ideas* lived.

is fully divine. Jesus is fully human." Maybe Peter would've agreed with all of them, and told Jesus so. "That's good to know," I could imagine Jesus saying in response to Peter, and turning to walk away. "Have a nice day. Enjoy your salvation."

As silly as that kind of speculative story is, consider how common this kind of belief is today. Think for a moment about the times you may have heard someone say they believe in Jesus and even espouse all the right ideas about Jesus, only to walk in ways that are contrary to the particular way of his life. We cannot simply have the right ideas in mind about him and call that belief. While that might work for gods who remain distant and undefined, the God who became particular flesh and chose to dwell among us became very particular and, in the process, redefined *belief* (John 1:14).

If the Word remained abstract—a mere idea floating above our in-the-flesh world—then perhaps belief could be the intellectual activity of agreeing with an idea. But the Word became flesh as a particular man who invited his followers to follow him in a particular way.[6] Jesus didn't ask that group of fishermen if they had the right ideas in mind about him. He invited them to follow. And when they followed, they were following a very particular person.

Christian faith is not merely an ideology, for the simple reason that the God of Christianity became flesh and asked us to follow him in our flesh. Belief in Jesus, then, is not a set of ideas about him that can be stated and defended by any means possible. Rather, belief is the act of following him in ways that are consistent with his way, trusting that the particular pattern of his life reveals to us truth beyond ideas and reality beyond propositions.

There is, then, an aspect of walking the path of particularity that cannot escape what Christians have, for generations, referred to as "the scandal of particularity." This is probably a more difficult challenge for those of us whose lives are consistently made more comfortable by the old ways. Often, the particularity of Jesus lands uncomfortably upon the lifestyles of

---

6. Talking about following the particular way of Jesus presents interesting challenges for those who are following his way two thousand years after he lived. Indeed, we cannot simply replicate each and every decision Jesus made or activity he enacted. Each and every community of Christians will need to discern how to follow the particular path of Jesus in their given context and culture. For more on this, I recommend Allen Verhey's reflections on discernment in *Remembering Jesus* (Grand Rapids: Eerdmans, 2005).

those who are most comfortable. In that case, the temptation to abandon his particular way for a more domesticated version of faith in Jesus will be alluring—especially the temptation to reduce his way to an ideology.

The scandal of particularity does not signal to followers of Jesus that they are called to create or seek out scandals; rather, the term "scandal of particularity" speaks more to the recognition that the act of following a particular person sometimes makes scandals unavoidable. Jesus's prophetic cry was a redemptive scandal to the prevailing religious sensibilities of his day, and it continues to be so in our time. His priestly presence scandalously mediated God to humans in ways previously unthinkable. His kingship, a political scandal of the highest order, did not signal that he was a new king in an existing political system but that he ushered in a new system of politics altogether—while wearing a crown of thorns.

Following the particular way of Jesus means that his way probably won't be compatible with other ways because of how different it is, and that's what makes it so redemptive. The more we follow the particular way of Jesus, the more his way will put us at odds with all of the other ways out there. The Gospel accounts acknowledge this reality, with Matthew going so far as to remind us that Jesus tells his disciples that following him may put them at odds with even their own family members (10:32–42). In fact, the historical situation in which the Gospels were written included some amount of resistance to the fledgling religious movement, not because of what its adherents thought but because of how they put it into practice with such exacting particularity.

Walking the path of particularity will mean taking the pattern of Jesus's life seriously enough to learn how to walk in that pattern through the varied contexts of modern life. The path of particularity calls for more than simply attempting to replicate first-century words and actions twenty centuries later. Each community of disciples will need to take up the challenge of learning to walk Jesus's way in the midst of their own, unique situations. This is not to say that the particularity of Jesus can be dismissed in the name of contextualization. Neither does affirming the particularity of Jesus dismiss the contextualized situation of each community. Every follower and community of followers will need to learn anew how the particularity of Jesus shapes the way life is to be lived in a given context, guided by the Holy Spirit.[7]

Walking the particular path of Jesus as we understand him to be a prophet, a priest, and a king will be the prevailing challenge in this book. The particular way of Jesus offers salvation because it saves us from all other ways that offer more of the same. In other words, Jesus fulfills the role of prophet, redeems the role of priest, and saves the role of king by the particular way he takes up each of those roles. The challenge for us comes in our response to the particular way he takes up and redefines each of those roles. Perhaps the way he does so will fit our expectations. Perhaps it won't. Either way, the challenge before us is to take a careful look at how he does his prophetic, priestly, and kingly work, and to take the steps to follow him in that way, wherever he may lead.

---

7. In addition to Allen Verhey's work on discernment (see previous note), I also recommend Sarah Coakley's book on the Holy Spirit's work as it draws communities into redemptive realities. See *God, Sexuality, and the Self: An Essay 'On the Trinity'* (Cambridge: Cambridge University Press, 2013).

2 ✝ FOLLOWING JESUS AS PROPHET

Timothy Green

AS JESUS and his followers came into Caesarea Philippi, he asked them who the crowds were saying that he was. They responded that some said he was John the Baptist, others Elijah, and others Jeremiah or one of the other prophets.[1] Of all of the possible confessions regarding Jesus's identity, why would the crowds have concluded he was a prophet? What was Jesus saying or doing that would indicate a prophetic identity? Are readers of the biblical texts to conclude that Jesus was a prophet based on the confused crowd's confession? In order for us to appreciate why the people would affirm him as a prophet, it is appropriate for us to take a step back into our ancient Israelite ancestors' perception of a prophet.

The Prophet in Ancient Israel's Tradition

When we hear the word "prophet" today, perhaps our first thought is of someone who has supernatural visions of future events. The concept may conjure up images of a person who provides divine answers to challenging questions. The term may evoke the notion of a social reformer who boldly challenges political, economic, and judicial structures and practices. Our ancient Israelite ancestors would not necessarily have excluded these ideas from their perception of a prophet. They had access to terminology for persons who had divinely inspired visions (*hozeh*, "visionary") as well as for persons capable of providing divine answers to problematic questions (*ro'eh*, "seer"). However, none of these concepts are the distinguishing mark for the prophets of the Old Testament.

---

1. See Matt. 16:14; Mark 8:28; Luke 9:19. In their accounts of the confusion over Jesus's identity, the Gospels repeat the same misunderstanding King Herod expressed (Mark 6:15; Luke 9:8).

In articulating the role of the prophet, our biblical ancestors consistently use the word *nabi'*. Toward the end of the call of Moses in Exodus 4, we gain insight into what this term essentially means. Arguing that he is unable to speak, Moses requests that the LORD[2] send someone else to speak to Pharaoh and the people (Exod. 4:10–13). The LORD will provide Aaron, Moses's brother (v. 14). As Moses puts his own words into Aaron's mouth, Aaron will speak the words for Moses. Aaron will serve as Moses's mouth (literally *nabi'*), and Moses will serve as God for Aaron (v. 16). The *nabi'* (prophet) is essentially one who has words put into their mouth so they can speak those words to others. Thus, the *nabi'* is the mouthpiece or spokesperson who delivers the message of another.

Because the prophet is called and sent by the LORD to speak the divine message to the covenant community, prophetic narratives often include the divine command, "Go and say . . ." The biblical prophets employ language used by ancient royal messengers as they introduce the LORD's message ("This is what the LORD says") and as they deliver their message in the first person, as if the originator of the message were actually speaking.

The Prophet and the Divine Word

Essential to the prophetic message is the actual *word* spoken by the prophet. For the sake of the covenant community, the prophet was entrusted with discerning and speaking the divine word (Hebrew, *dabar*), just as the priest was entrusted with *Torah* (instruction) and the wise person with wise counsel.[3] The divine word in the mouth of the prophets had a formational and evocative, even creative or destructive, capacity in the life of the community. The term *dabar* carries with it a double nuance, meaning both "word" and "thing." The *word* received and spoken inherently contains and engenders the very *thing* spoken through the word. The *word* becomes the *thing*.[4]

---

2. The use of small caps—both here and in many translations of the Bible—indicates the divine name YHWH (often written as Yahweh in English). When Lord is written this way, it represents the special, divine name of Israel's God, which Jewish people will not say aloud.

3. See this threefold breakdown of the social responsibility of the priests, the sages, and the prophets in Jer. 18:18.

4. While the spoken word is the primary mode by which the prophet delivered the divine message, on various occasions prophets delivered the message through symbolic acts or even miraculous signs. Miraculous signs are rare in the biblical prophets; however, the

The call narrative of Jeremiah poignantly demonstrates the transformative and evocative power of the prophetic word (Jer. 1). In response to Jeremiah's objection that he does not know how to speak (*dabar*), the LORD announces that he has put his words into the prophet's mouth.[5] That divine-prophetic word will have both deconstructive and constructive capabilities: "to pluck up and to pull down, to destroy and to overthrow, to build and to plant" (v. 10, NRSV). The God from whom this word originates commits Godself to watch over the word and ultimately "to perform it" (v. 12, NRSV; i.e., to materialize the word spoken).

The Prophetic Message

So what, then, was the message spoken by the Old Testament prophets? What did the prophetic word say and do? Each prophet's unique background, vocabulary, and even personality influenced the manner in which the message was communicated. The specific historical and social situation into which each prophet spoke provided the context that shaped the prophet's message. However, in spite of the uniqueness of each prophet's message, the conviction that consistently engendered all prophetic messages was that a covenant bond existed between the LORD and his people. "I will be your God, and you will be my people" informed prophetic messages of both judgment and salvation, calls to repentance and utterances of hope.[6] Through prophetic words and deeds, prophets called the community to remember the LORD's covenant fidelity toward them. Prophets challenged the community to embody that same covenant fidelity toward the LORD and each other.[7]

---

narratives of Elijah and Elisha depict the prophets as carrying them out. Certain acts of Elisha echo into the ministry of Jesus (raising the Shunammite's son from the dead, feeding one hundred persons from twenty loves of barley, and healing of the leper Naaman; see 2 Kings 4–5).

5. See Jer. 1:9. A similar account of ingesting the divine word occurs in Ezek. 2:8–3:4 as the prophet digests the scroll handed to him by the LORD and then receives the divine directive to "go to the house of Israel and speak my very words to them" (3:4, NRSV).

6. For examples of this refrain, see Gen. 17:8; Exod. 6:7; 29:45; Lev. 26:12; Jer. 30:22; Ezek. 14:11; Hosea 2:23; and Zech. 8:8.

7. Many prophetic books contain sections of messages directed toward the nations. For example, see Isa. 13–23; Jer. 46–51; Ezek. 25–32; and Amos 1:3–2:3, as well as the books of Obadiah and Nahum.

In seasons of the people's covenant infidelity toward God and toward neighbor, the prophetic message spoke judgment, deconstructed abusive power, critiqued worship practices that were divorced from socioeconomic practices, and called the community to repentance. The prophetic word frequently found itself unabashedly criticizing the misuse and abuse of power that was legitimized by the national religion and embodied in political, economic, judicial, and religious systems. Prophets spoke with resolute honesty to the leaders of the community, condemning self-serving power, social and economic brutalities, legal injustices, and religious syncretism. The prophet's message often resulted in direct confrontations with rulers, elders who made judicial decisions at the city gate, self-serving priests who fed on the people's infatuation with public displays of sacrifice, and prophets who spoke empty words of peace desired by the masses.

The prophet Elijah serves as a prototype for prophetic confrontation of abuses by the royal power[8] and with the popular gods of the day. As the prophetic voice cried out divine truth to structures of abusive and self-serving power, that voice was readily labeled a troublemaker (1 Kings 18:17). Likewise, as the prophet Jeremiah delivered the divine message through word and deed, he repeatedly found himself in direct conflict with and in a defensive posture against the very centers of power, from kings to priests to fellow prophets (Jer. 26:16). Ultimately, Jeremiah's temple sermon evoked such wrath of the religious leaders (priests and prophets) that they sought to kill him (v. 11).[9] Surprisingly, the political officials and "all the people" disagreed that Jeremiah should be killed. They concluded, "This man does not deserve the sentence of death" (v. 16, NRSV).[10]

To understand the prophetic word solely in terms of critique, deconstruction, and judgment, however, is to ignore the essential other side. In situations of desolation and despair, the prophetic message becomes one of salvation and hope. The same prophets who uttered a word of condemnation in seasons of oppression, violence, and infidelity became proclaimers of a word of restoration in seasons of barrenness and death. The prophetic message dared to imagine and engender the people's imagination of an alternative reality to

---

8. See especially the narrative of Naboth's vineyard in 1 Kings 21.

9. See also Amos's confrontation with the priest Amaziah in Amos 7:10–17.

10. For more context, see the temple sermon of Jeremiah and its effects on various groups in the community in chapters 7 and 26.

the life-taking reign of the empire. Grounded in the LORD's covenant faithfulness to his people, the divine word inspired a hope-filled future.[11]

Jesus as Prophet

In light of the primary task of the prophet as messenger of the LORD through both word and deed that prompted conflict with the powers and engendered hope for those in despair, it comes as no surprise that crowds might have viewed Jesus as a prophet. Perhaps some even would have viewed Jesus as *the* prophet anticipated from the time of Moses, the prophet *par excellence* by whom all other prophets were measured. Israel's prophetic tradition[12] anticipated that the LORD would raise up a prophet (or prophets) like Moses: "I will put my words in the mouth of the prophet, who shall speak to them everything that I command" (Deut. 18:18, NRSV).[13]

All four Gospels depict the crowds or various individuals confessing that Jesus is a (perhaps *the*) prophet. Early in the Gospel of John, Philip announces to Nathanael, "We have found him about whom Moses in the law and also the prophets wrote" (1:45, NRSV).[14] Later on, in Jesus's conversation with the Samaritan woman, she responds to him with the simple declaration, "Sir, I see that you are a prophet" (4:19, NRSV). For John, Jesus's miraculous signs are interpreted by some as pointing to his prophetic status. Following the feeding of five thousand, the crowds declare that Jesus is "indeed the prophet

---

11. Particularly, the prophetic word in the season of exile spoke of a reversal from death to life, despair to hope, barrenness to fertility. See Jer. 29–33; Ezek. 33–39; the restoration of the temple in Ezek. 40–48; and Isa. 40–55.

12. The prophetic tradition is articulated particularly in the book of Deuteronomy and continues in the division of the Hebrew Bible known as the Prophets, comprised of the Former Prophets (Joshua, Judges, 1 and 2 Samuel, 1 and 2 Kings) and the Latter Prophets (Isaiah, Jeremiah, Ezekiel, the Twelve).

13. The Old Testament narratives of the call of Jeremiah and the ministry of Elijah are depicted as parallels to Moses. The prophet Malachi emphasizes a prophet to come in the line of Elijah (4:5). The Gospels' portrayal of John the Baptist in the wilderness picks up on this prophetic tradition as well. Following the healing of the lame man, Peter quotes the words of Moses: "The Lord your God will raise up for you from your own people a prophet like me. You must listen to whatever he tells you" (Acts 3:22, NRSV). See the same reference in Stephen's sermon (Acts 7:37).

14. When the priests and Levites question John the Baptist's identity, John the Baptist confesses that he was not the Messiah nor Elijah nor the prophet (John 1:19–28).

---

who is to come into the world" (6:14, NRSV).[15] Upon Jesus's invitation to the thirsty to come to him and drink, John reports that some in the crowd conclude, "This is really the prophet" (7:37, 40, NRSV).[16] Again, when the Pharisees ask the blind man healed by Jesus what he has to say about Jesus, he concisely responds, "He is a prophet" (9:17).

As Jesus enters into Jerusalem to shouts of "Hosanna to the Son of David," Matthew states that people began to ask who this Jesus was. Some respond, "This is the prophet Jesus from Nazareth in Galilee" (21:9, 11, NRSV).[17] Likewise, Luke recounts that, after Jesus brought the deceased son of the widow back to life, the crowd praised God and declared, "A great prophet has risen among us" (7:16, NRSV). Luke also recounts that, on the way to Emmaus, the two followers of Jesus describe Jesus as "a prophet mighty in deed and word before God and all the people" (24:19, NRSV).[18] Certainly, a common trait throughout the Gospel narratives is the association between Jesus's evocative words and mighty deeds and his identification as a prophet.

Beyond a Prophet

The provocative words of Jesus, accompanied by his miraculous deeds, would have led some to conclude that Jesus followed in the line of Elijah, Jeremiah, or one of the other prophets. His critiques of abusive power and religious exclusivity are reminiscent of prophets such as Amos, Micah, and

---

15. In the Gospel of John, after the people see the feeding of the five thousand they attempt to make Jesus their king.

16. Likewise, others testify that Jesus was the Messiah (John 7:41).

17. Immediately after this, Jesus denounces the traders in the temple, declaring words reminiscent of Jeremiah's temple sermon. See also Matt. 21:45–46, in which the chief priests and Pharisees refrained from arresting Jesus because they were afraid of those who regarded Jesus as a prophet.

18. While the crowds and individuals esteemed Jesus as a prophet, neither he himself nor any of the Gospel writers directly proclaim him a prophet. Perhaps one of the closest instances to his self-identification as a prophet occurs in his hometown of Nazareth, when he comments that "no prophet is accepted in the prophet's hometown" (Luke 4:24, NRSV). He proceeds to describe Elijah's ministry to the widow at Zarephath and Elisha's healing of Naaman the Syrian. His statement, however, is less a confession that he is a prophet and more a hint about the nature of his ministry (like that of Elijah and Elisha) to those outside the Jewish community. As a result, the townspeople of Nazareth reject him to the point of attempting to throw him off a cliff.

Isaiah. His inspiring and imaginative depictions of a kingdom turned upside down recall the hope-filled messages of the exilic prophets. However, the Gospel narratives are insistent that what Jesus was doing was not merely critiquing and judging the present powers. He was not merely speaking of a future in which God would destroy the present empire and establish his reign on earth. Rather, he was himself enacting the overthrow of abusive and self-serving powers. He was casting out the violent and oppressive forces before the crowds' eyes. He himself was embodying the alternative way of being on earth and establishing the very reign of God on earth.

Jesus spoke prophetic words, pronounced prophetic judgments, envisioned prophetic hope, and inspired prophetic imagination for generations to come. However, he is not simply another messenger who spoke a word from God. As the prologue to the Gospel of John declares, this Jesus *is* the Word of God (1:1). That which prophets of the past have spoken has become flesh and blood in Jesus. We have not only heard the word of God, but we have also seen it with our eyes and touched it with our hands (1 John 1:1–3).

Though Jesus proclaimed image-laden prophetic words and carried out mightily prophetic deeds, his call was not to reform the present kingdom but, rather, to follow him in his establishment of a new reality—the kingdom of God. His miraculous signs were not simply for the authentication of his ministry or for the validation of his message. His deeds were establishing a kingdom where the blind see, debts are canceled, prisoners are released, hungry are fed, sinners are forgiven, foreigners become family members, and a life-giving, grace-filled table is prepared.

While the words and deeds of Jesus have rightly led many to understand and even confess that Jesus is a prophet, the entirety of the Gospel narrative refuses to stop short at that confession. Jesus's continued probing of his disciples makes clear that the Gospel story compels disciples of Jesus to follow him on the way, all the way to his final destination. On the way, he not only will ask us, "Who do people say I am?" He continues his interrogation by asking us, "Who do you say I am?" In this journey, Jesus disciples his followers into recognizing that he has not come to reform the world but has come to establish the reign of God, where all things are made new and where the divine will is carried out on earth just as it is in heaven. Somewhere along that journey, like Peter, we too discover: "You are the Messiah, the Son of the living God."

3 ✝ FOLLOWING JESUS WITH PROPHETIC IMAGINATION

Stephanie Smith Matthews

PROPHETS see and speak out against injustices in society that others fail to recognize. They receive visions, speak through oracles and parables, and intentionally use their bodies in symbolic acts. These unusual activities tend to grab attention and can lead to confusion or anger. Prophets are ridiculed, ignored, injured by violence, and even killed. The few who listen to them long and hard enough will discover a message of radical hope for a society transformed by divine justice.

This chapter will draw on the testimony of three prophets who exemplified living and speaking with prophetic imagination. The Old Testament prophet Zechariah, whose prophetic activity is recorded in the book bearing his name, was active when Jerusalem's walls were still a pile of rubble from their defeat by a foreign army.[1] Matthew's Gospel celebrates Jesus as standing within and fulfilling the line of prophets like Zechariah. And Martin Luther King, Jr.—a man broadly celebrated by U.S. society and still revered by many Christians—is a prophet whose witness is worth considering among the likes of Zechariah and Jesus Christ.

Prophecy is a communal activity. Prophets point out injustice *in the community*. They are particularly concerned with the relationship between people who enjoy certain power, privileges, or wealth and those who do not. In terms of biblical prophecy, prophets communicate a God-given message

---

1. Traditionally, Zechariah is said to have returned from Babylon to Jerusalem with the exiles and to have begun his prophetic career around 520 BCE.

to the world. They bring truth—sometimes uncomfortable truth—from God's perspective to communities that claim to live for God. Prophets speak and act *in front of the community*, directing their proclamations toward those who perpetuate injustice by grasping tightly to their wealth, power, or privilege. The hopeful vision prophets cast is one of a *transformed community*. Unfortunately, the suffering that so many prophets are made to endure comes *at the hands of the community* by those who refuse to accept their message. Too often, communities deny the truth of a prophecy as well as its divine origin.

See the Reality of Injustice in Society

One obstacle between many of us and our prophetic voice is the improper assumption that prophecy is peripheral to Christian life. The repeated call to take up our cross and follow Christ (Matt. 10:38; 16:24; Mark 8:34; Luke 9:23; 14:27) includes taking on his prophetic imagination: his way of seeing the world around him. We cannot remain locked in familiar patterns of thinking. We have to be willing to allow the Holy Spirit to radically change our perspectives of our society, our churches, and ourselves.

Pray. *Lord, I believe. Help my unbelief. Grant me the courage to hear your difficult truths from those who see things differently than I do. Help me to lay down my pride and accept that I could be wrong.*

Reflect. *Am I listening to the entire gospel, or just the part about my individual salvation?* The full gospel unveiled in Scripture proclaims a God who desires to transform communities into centers of economic justice. Many of the Old Testament laws were set in place to protect those left vulnerable in society. Old Testament prophets like Zechariah championed the same message: "Thus says the LORD of hosts: Render true judgments, enact covenantal faithfulness and compassion, each one to another. The widow, the orphan, the immigrant, and the poor do not oppress" (Zech. 7:9–10a, author's translation).[2] Time and time again, Jesus sided with the poor over those with wealth, power, and privilege. His advice to the rich man who so desperately desired to be personally righteous was to give his wealth to the

---

2. All Scripture quotations in this chapter are the author's own translation.

poor.[3] This biblical message of justice calls us to loosen our grip on what we think we have earned but which ultimately comes from God.

Practice. Make yourself aware of the realities of injustice in your community. Where are there disparities among school resources, access to medical care, good housing, jobs, and transportation to those jobs? What is the history behind these situations? Sometimes inequality is so rooted in a community's history that its citizens lose sight of all the factors that have been involved in creating unjust societies.

Questions such as these do not have easy answers or obvious solutions. Learn from those who are further along than you are on the journey of following Jesus with prophetic imagination. Seek out prophetic voices among minsters, civic leaders, and grassroots organizers. These prophetic leaders have research, reports, and anecdotal evidence that can open your eyes to the truths about your community. Listen deeply to those with whom you are prone to disagree. Sit with differing opinions—even if, at first, you can't understand the perspective.

There is privilege in having the choice to listen to discomforting, dissenting voices or to ignore them and keep on living as we always have. Mary Rearick Paul has explained this privilege in a chapter of her book poignantly titled "The Toxicity of Power": "Studies have consistently shown that where there is disparity in power, the underclass knows and understands much more about the lives and workings of those who have power than those with power know about them. This knowledge is a basic underclass necessity for survival. For those in power, understanding the perspective of others was never necessary and therefore a highly underdeveloped skill."[4] Lay down the privilege that allows you the freedom to focus on yourself and your own experiences, and humbly seek the divine image reflected in all people.

These were the very issues Martin Luther King Jr. addressed in "Letter from a Birmingham Jail," written to eight moderate, white religious leaders.

---

3. This story appears in the Synoptic Gospels (Matt. 19:16–30; Mark 10:17–31; and Luke 18:18–30). In Matthew's account, the man who approaches Jesus is said to be both rich and young. In Mark's account, he is described merely as wealthy. As Luke tells it, the man is a wealthy ruler. In a conflation of the three accounts, Christians often refer to Jesus's conversation partner as "the rich, young ruler."

4. Mary Rearick Paul, *Women Who Lead: The Call of Women in Ministry* (Kansas City: Beacon Hill Press of Kansas City, 2011), 85.

He wrote to open their eyes to how very differently they viewed the reality of the struggle for civil rights:

I had the strange feeling when I was suddenly catapulted into the leadership of the bus protest in Montgomery several years ago that we would have the support of the white church. I felt that the white ministers, priests, and rabbis of the South would be some of our strongest allies. Instead, some few have been outright opponents, refusing to understand the freedom movement and misrepresenting its leaders; all too many others have been more cautious than courageous and have remained silent behind the anesthetizing security of stained-glass windows.

In spite of my shattered dreams of the past, I came to Birmingham with the hope that the white religious leadership of this community would see the justice of our cause and with deep moral concern serve as the channel through which our just grievances could get to the power structure. I had hoped that each of you would understand. But again I have been disappointed.[5]

King's deep disappointment with white religious leaders is palpable throughout the pages of this letter. These leaders were left with the choice to be defensive or to believe the testimony of one who directly experienced racial injustice in their society. More than half a century later, Christians continue to struggle with the call to lay down the privilege of our own perspectives. In order to have our eyes opened to the reality of injustice around us, we must *acknowledge* whatever power and privilege we hold, and humbly *accept* corrective words from others.

Reflect. *Where do I benefit from privilege, and where don't I? If this letter were written today, would it be addressed to me?* Gaining new perspectives on injustice can be personal and overwhelming. Find conversation partners in fellow church members, friends, family, and mentors. Ask questions—but at this stage, talk less and listen more. Keep in mind that the point of this journey of personal transformation is not just a life-changing experience that benefits you. God's prophetic vision is that the community will be transformed through personal transformation.

---

5. Martin Luther King Jr., "Letter from a Birmingham Jail," April 16, 1963.

Pray. *God, help me to resist shutting down or giving up when I become overwhelmed. Open my eyes to the prophets through whom you are speaking in my community.*

Proclaim the Reality of Injustice in Society

Nobody was ever called a prophet who kept quietly to themselves. Prophets speak out! Prophets act! Prophets do what is necessary to shift their community members' gaze from their complacency to injustices among them. Following Jesus with prophetic imagination means we too name injustice when we see it in society, in our churches, and in ourselves.

Do not wait for a "perfect" opportunity to begin speaking out. Demands for a flawless message, delivered in flawless fashion, by a flawless human being are not only unreasonable; they also deflect attention away from the prophetic message. Speak judiciously, guided by the Spirit, and accept that you will make mistakes. Continue listening for prophetic voices that can serve as a corrective along the way.

Practice. Start by confessing where injustice is evident in your personal life and dealings with others. Admit where you are the beneficiary of unjust policies or unfair opportunities. You may feel uncomfortable drawing attention to yourself in this way. The purpose of speaking out, after all, is ultimately about drawing attention to injustice, not to oneself. But prophetic activity always draws *some* attention to oneself. As King made clear in his letter, the intent of prophetic acts of protest is to awaken those who remain stubbornly blind to injustice. Do not let someone else's manner of drawing attention distract you from the message they are proclaiming; it may very well be the voice of God!

Reflect. *Through whom can God be expected to speak? What do I expect a minister to look like? Does my church community squelch the Spirit by unfairly privileging some voices over others?* No one is the expert of every form of injustice in their community. Just because you have become aware of an issue does not mean you have to become its sole spokesperson. In many cases, people directly experiencing the negative effects of an injustice have already been speaking out about it for a long time. A prophet's role includes pointing out the voice of God in others. Validate what others are saying, showing that you have chosen to believe them, and that others in the community should as well. John the Baptist, himself a prophet, spent his ministry pointing the way to Jesus (e.g., Matt. 3:11). A common way for

Christian artists to depict John the Baptist is with an outstretched finger pointing to the figure of Jesus. John drew attention to himself through his speech, how he dressed, and what he ate. Yet, when the spotlight burned brightest on him, he chose to amplify the voice of God in another prophet, who established a way for justice to be the hallmark of God's people.

Practice. Affirm what others have said and done, and mention them by name. Work with local church leaders to invite experts on a particular issue to speak in your church. Position yourself visibly up front if the speaker will represent a minority voice to your congregation based on ethnicity, gender, socioeconomic status, or any other marker. Confess, if necessary, that not everyone in your congregation may be willing to accept the message, which will allow the potential speaker to discern whether they are truly called to speak to your context at that time. Encourage others to join you in sitting under the leadership of these experts outside the comfort of your own church.

God often asks a prophet to speak before others are ready to heed the message. Inevitably, only a few choose to listen. In Matthew 13:10, the disciples asked Jesus why he spoke in parables. What they seem to be asking is, "Why do you package your message in such a strange way? Why not change the way you communicate so that more people might accept it?" Jesus responded that he was fulfilling a prophecy from Isaiah 6:9–10 (see Matt. 13:13–15). His interpretation of these verses shows that he did not expect everyone who listened to him to be willing to accept his message, no matter how he communicated it. The same is true for us: no matter how skillfully we speak out about injustice, some will simply refuse to believe us. If we follow Jesus with prophetic imagination, it may mean others will reject us, along with the message of God's full gospel.

We are left to trust in God to do the work of transformation ultimately. We can do great harm when we try to control or manipulate others into doing what we think is best. Using our collective strength as a community, we can forge the Bible into a weapon that drives people away from God, instead of offering it as an invitation to meet with God in community. Though Jesus often spoke forcefully to religious leaders about their need to change, he never used his role as a prophet to force anyone to act against their will. In fact, the Christian doctrine of free will teaches us that fundamental to God's character is the laying down of control over us and allowing us either to accept or reject a relationship with God. Release the need for control over others. If God can grant us free will, we should do the same for others.

Pray. *May your Spirit stir me from my complacency and give me the courage to speak out about injustice. Reveal specific ways I can amplify your voice that I have come to hear in others.*

Cast God's Hopeful Vision for a Just Society

Prophecy is not all doom and gloom. Yes, biblical prophets call attention to what is wrong with the world. Those with ears to hear the prophetic message rightly lament the brokenness in their world. But the beauty of the prophetic imagination is in the ability to envision a new reality into which God is calling us through the voice of prophets, one in which justice prevails in society, enabling God's people to live peaceably with one another.

The hopeful vision in Zechariah 8 begins with God's promise to dwell in Jerusalem. God's presence would accompany a new reality: "Thus says the LORD of hosts: Old men and old women will again sit along the streets of Jerusalem, some with walking staff in hand due to old age" (v. 4). In other words, life would be so protected from warfare, famine, and disease that people would once again live to a ripe old age. The vision continues in verse 5: "And the streets of the city will be filled with boys and girls playing in its streets." What a joyful vision!

Sometimes, though, deep pain surfaces from the specificity of new visions. Compare Zechariah's vision to Lamentations 2, penned just seventy years earlier about those same streets. The latter half of this song of lament spills out fresh grief over the loss of children through forced starvation when Jerusalem was under siege by the Babylonians: "Lift your palms to [the Lord] for the lives of your children who are faint from hunger at the head of every street" (v. 19b). Had these children survived, they would have been old men and women by the time Zechariah began prophesying. Instead, Zechariah's new vision is haunted by the memory of lives tragically cut short: "They lie on the ground in the streets, young and old. Young women and young men have fallen by the sword" (v. 21a). There are times in which we can't bear to renew our hope because the pain of unrealized hopes has been too great a burden to bear. In our prophetic message of hope, let us proceed with sensitivity, and make room for lament.

Pray. *Lord, grant me the sensitivity to perceive when casting a vision of hope will bring pain. Help us to make room in our hearts and in our churches for lament.*

The premise of the prophets' message, reflected in our incarnational Christian theology, is that God's kingdom breaks into our world. God became flesh to serve—and, in some ways, become—the least of these. Jesus said, in fulfillment of the prophecy found in Isaiah 61, that the Spirit of the Lord had anointed him "to bring good news to the poor . . . to proclaim release to the captives and recovery of sight to the blind, to free the oppressed, to proclaim the year of the Lord's favor" (Luke 4:18). The Old Testament prophets demanded that justice reign on earth. Old Testament laws guided a particular society toward greater economic justice. Even as we await the ultimate fulfillment of God's kingdom in the age to come, our biblical mandate is to work toward a just society now, in accordance with the vision God has given of the kind of people we are supposed to be.

Prophetic visions seem radical, even reckless, because of how different they are from our present reality. Martin Luther King Jr.'s "I Have a Dream" speech from 1963 is certainly one of the most recognized speeches in U.S. history. King continued dreaming up radical visions of a transformed society in the last five years of his life, before his assassination. In 1967, he cast a vision of economic justice in the U.S. that may sound radical even fifty years later.[6] As much as most of us would like to believe we would have stood with King, I am persuaded that the vast majority of Americans would have dismissed his vision for the U.S. economy as too reckless. But prophets like King have not failed to recognize obstacles between the current reality and their radical visions. Radical prophets acknowledge obstacles fully but refuse to let them be the last word. They inspire others to work together for creative solutions to the obstacles that stand between us and a just society.

Prophets always remember the powerful one whose message they proclaim. Following his interaction with the rich, young ruler, Jesus told his disciples how difficult it is for the wealthy to enter the kingdom of God. The disciples, incredulous, asked Jesus how anyone could be saved. Jesus looked them in the face and said, "For humanity this is impossible, but for God all is possible" (Matt. 19:26). Once again, Jesus echoed an Old Testament prophet: "Thus says the LORD of hosts: Though it is impossible in your eyes, the remnant of the people in these days, is it also impossible in my eyes? declares the LORD of hosts" (Zech. 8:6). God heard the laments of

---

6. To read King's economic vision, see Martin Luther King Jr., "Where We Are Going" in *Where Do We Go from Here: Chaos or Community?* (Boston: Beacon Press, 2010).

a grieving people and encouraged them that God could do what they could not envision. May we be reminded that ours is a God who casts visions of hope into seemingly hopeless situations.

Pray. *Creator God, who forms order out of chaos, in your mercy grant new visions to us all. Help us to hold on to the hope of transformation when all we can see is brokenness.*

Prepare for Suffering and Loss at the Hands of Society

Jesus and John the Baptist were executed. So were Old Testament prophets. Countless others have met with death because of their prophetic witness. Martin Luther King Jr. was assassinated within a year of writing about his vision of economic justice. For years before his murder, King lived with violence and threats of violence against him and his family. Prophets who have escaped violence have been ostracized by their community, rejected by those not willing to hear.

Not all will listen, especially when the message demands that the privileged and the wealthy lay down their privilege and wealth for the sake of justice. The radical new reality of a just society is a threat to those who benefit from society being unjust. The rich, young ruler is but one example. Note the people's response to Zechariah's call for economic justice: "They refused to listen and hardened their hearts against the law and prophets God sent by the Spirit" (7:11–12a). Think for a moment of the dangerous lengths public leaders go to in order to hide painful truths—even from themselves—for the sake of protecting their image of power. Unprotected prophets take great risk when speaking truth to power.

Practice. Before assuming the role of a prophet, look inward and confess when you have ostracized or otherwise wounded God's prophets, or when you have stood back and said nothing while others ostracized or wounded them.

Start living into discomfort. We prepare ourselves for more difficult tests through the discipline of consistent practice. If asked to volunteer to do something that makes you uncomfortable, say yes, and ask for help when you need it.

Speak up when someone else is treated unfairly. If those who do not risk much by speaking up refuse to do so, how can they ask it of those for whom the risk is great?

Prepare for loss. Tell loved ones why you are speaking out and acting differently. Set up a support network of people who will help care for you when you begin to pay the price of prophetic activity. Cultivate practices of self-care, including time for lament before God and others. Discern through prayer and conversation with mentors the level of risk to which you are called.

Reflect. *What do I fear will happen if I speak and live with prophetic imagination? What holds me back?*

Pray. *Jesus, grant me the ability risk joining you in suffering.*

If you choose to follow Jesus with prophetic imagination, you will find yourself led to a life of prophetic speech and activity. Because our words and actions are only prophetic insomuch as they proclaim the vision of God, they must be discerned through prayer. Root yourself in God's idea of justice as proclaimed throughout both Testaments of the Bible. Make the effort to see the reality of the injustices permeating society, the church, and yourself. Under the guidance of the Spirit, speak out against these injustices, especially by amplifying the voices of others who need to be heard most. Prepare for the suffering, lament, resistance, and dissent that are to be expected responses to prophetic proclamation. And risk taking hold of God's radically peaceable vision of communities transformed by justice.

Suggestions for Further Reading

Goizueta, Roberto S. "Hacia una Teología de Acompañamiento" in *Caminemos con Jesús: Toward a Hispanic/Latino Theology of Accompaniment*. Maryknoll, NY: Orbis Books, 1995.

Jung, L. Shannon. *Building the Good Life for All: Transforming Income Inequality in our Communities*. Louisville: Westminster John Knox Press, 2017.

King, Martin Luther, Jr. "Letter from a Birmingham Jail." April 16, 1963.

____. "Three Dimensions of a Complete Life." Sermon preached at New Covenant Baptist Church, Chicago, April 9, 1976.

____. *Where Do We Go from Here: Chaos or Community?* Boston: Beacon Press, 2010.

Paul, Mary Rearick. *Women Who Lead: The Call of Women in Ministry*. Kansas City: Beacon Hill Press of Kansas City, 2011.

Smith-Christopher, Daniel. "Hearing Silenced Voices in the Bible: The Other Ten Commandments." In *Jonah, Jesus, and Other Good Coyotes: Speaking Peace to Power in the Bible*. Nashville: Abingdon Press, 2007.

4 ✝ FOLLOWING JESUS'S PROPHETIC WELCOME OF WOMEN

Kara Lyons-Pardue

THIS MUCH is certain: anywhere Jesus is surrounded by a group of followers, or anytime the generic term "disciples" (*mathētai*) appears in the narratives of the Gospels, we should assume that women were present in that company. But because *the Twelve* were men, and are offhandedly referred to as "the disciples" in our common speech, we may mistakenly envision a throng of only men accompanying Jesus.[1] Unfortunately, this misconception clouds what is apparent across the Gospels in varying ways: that Jesus's followers included women from the earliest days of his ministry in Galilee. Jesus's lived example functions prophetically, exemplifying the boundary-breaking gospel (Acts 2:16–21; Gal. 3:26–29) and illustrating God's very nature that should shape how Christians today treat one another. Jesus's welcome of women casts a prophetic vision for relationships and community set right in God's kingdom—a vision that challenges us even today.

---

1. John mentions the Twelve as a specific group among the disciples but does not list them. The first time John mentions this inner circle is 6:67, when—in light of many other followers turning away from him—Jesus asked the Twelve whether they also wished to leave. Simon Peter answered the question. Then John 6:70–71 acknowledges both the chosen status of the Twelve and Jesus's betrayer, Judas Iscariot, in their midst. Thomas is described as "one of the Twelve" (20:24). John only specifies these three as part of the Twelve in John, although it is reasonable that the disciples in the call narratives belong also to this group (see John 1:31–51).

Jesus's Prophetic Welcome of Women Disciples

Each Gospel includes indications that women were among Jesus's closest associates.[2] Taken in general, the collective testimony of the New Testament Gospels offers the Christian community a vision of Jesus prophetically forming a community faithful to God, in part, by welcoming women. In particular, these women disciples played a crucial role in relationship to Jesus's crucifixion, death, burial, and resurrection. Even the church's most notorious early critic, Celsus, who wrote to refute Christianity, noted pejoratively how central Jesus's female followers were to the resurrection witness: "The question is, whether any one who was really dead ever rose with a veritable body . . . that while alive [Jesus] was of no assistance to himself, but that when dead he rose again, and showed the marks of his punishment, and how his hands were pierced with nails: who beheld this? A half-frantic woman, as you state, and some other one, perhaps, of those who were engaged in the same system of delusion."[3] Celsus may be referring to John's account only (John 20:11–18) and pessimistically, at that. But each Gospel testifies that women were *the* key witnesses to these crucial moments of Jesus's life. The listed names of the women vary somewhat across the accounts, but among them, Mary Magdalene stands out as the foremost witness to Jesus's death and resurrection (Matt. 27:55–56, 61; 28:1–11; Mark 15:40–41, 47; 16:1, 9; Luke 24:9-11; John 19:25; 20:1–2, 11–18).[4]

One might ask: how did women followers become crucial witnesses to the crucifixion and resurrection if Jesus's twelve disciples were all men? The

---

2. Matt. 27:55–56; Mark 15:40–41; Luke 8:1–3; 10:38–42; 24:10; John 11:1–37; 19:25–27; 20:1–18.

3. Quoted in Origen, *Against Celsus* (*Ante-Nicene Fathers*, vol. 4; ed. A. Cleveland Coxe; Hendrickson, 1994), 2.55. Celsus was a second-century philosopher. His works survive only in quotation by the church father Origen, who writes to counter his claims. In the brief quotation included here, Celsus claims to be quoting a Jew, but many people subsequently have considered this character to be a literary device.

4. Luke reports that Mary Magdalene was a recipient of healing by Jesus, having been possessed by seven demons (8:2; see also Mark 16:9). Mary Magdalene is often confused for Mary of Bethany (sister of Martha and Lazarus)—especially in relation to the account in John 12:1–11—but these Marys are meant to be distinguished by the other identifiers (often place names). Tal Ilan's study of names in Palestine found that as many as 25 percent of women in this time period were named some variant of Mary. *Lexicon of Jewish Names in Late Antiquity: Part I, Palestine 330 BCE–200 CE* (Tübingen, Germany: Mohr Siebeck, 2002), 57.

Gospel according to Mark, which most scholars believe to be the earliest-written Gospel, describes Jesus's ministry in a rushed, urgent tone. Those in Jesus's company are described either as his "disciples" (*mathētai*; first in 2:15)[5] or "those who were around him" (3:34; 4:10, NRSV). This group of followers is distinct from the crowd (*ochlos*) that forms in different locations, apparently populated by locals who have heard about Jesus (3:20; 4:1).

By the time we reach Mark's lengthy passion narrative, Jesus has encountered many women—mostly anonymous or described only by their relationship to a named male—in the course of his healing and teaching ministry (e.g., 5:21–43; 14:1–11). We would have no clue, however, that women have been accompanying Jesus on his itinerant ministry until Mark mentions it after the crucifixion. After Jesus's final breath (15:37), the tearing of the temple curtain (v. 38), and centurion's exclamation (v. 39), Mark takes note of the scene in the vicinity of the cross: "There were also women looking on from a distance; among them were Mary Magdalene, and Mary the mother of James the younger and of Joses, and Salome. These used to follow him and provided for him when he was in Galilee; and there were many other women who had come up with him to Jerusalem" (15:40–41, NRSV). Those named women—Mary Magdalene, Mary the mother of James and Joses, and Salome—are mentioned again in various configurations in 15:47 and 16:1. The initial mention in 15:40–41 is a shocking revelation if we have imagined Jesus's ministry as a men-only road trip. As John Carroll says, "There has been a silent presence—or absence from the narration—until this retrospective aside."[6] In just two verses, Mark effectively inserts these named women and others into nearly all of the preced-

---

5. The term *mathētai* is used 46 times in Mark alone (233 times in the four Gospels together) The term generally refers to students or adherents. Those who sit under Jesus's teaching and seek to identify themselves with their teacher can be called disciples. Thus, the term "the disciples" refers to a larger group than the Twelve (*dōdeka*). In Mark 3:14, the Twelve are also called apostles. "Apostle" comes from the Greek *apostolos*, which is a compound noun indicating one who has been sent (*stellō*) out (*apo*). The term "apostles" appears only once more in Mark, again in reference to the Twelve (6:7), after the disciples return from their healing, preaching, exorcising mission (6:30).

6. John T. Carroll, *Jesus and the Gospels: An Introduction* (Louisville: Westminster John Knox, 2016), 82.

ing stories. These women have ministered (*diakoneō*)[7] to or with Jesus throughout his Galilean travels and up to Jerusalem, which makes them an essential part of the collective group of followers and disciples throughout Jesus's entire ministry. Similarly, Matthew's Gospel mentions only after the crucifixion that women have been there all along (Matt. 27:55–56).[8]

Luke's contribution to this portrait of Jesus's female followers is substantial. Luke names some women in Jesus's company much earlier in his ministry: "After this, Jesus traveled about from one town and village to another, proclaiming the good news of the kingdom of God. The Twelve were with him, and also some women who had been cured of evil spirits and diseases: Mary (called Magdalene) from whom seven demons had come out; Joanna the wife of Chuza, the manager of Herod's household; Susanna; and many others. These women were helping to support them out of their own means" (8:1–3). Luke names only Mary Magdalene, Joanna, and Susanna but states that there were "many others." These women are not mere groupies; they seem to have been important funders of Jesus's mission at the very least, based on the reference to "their own means."

The NIV's language of "helping" is not quite accurate in Luke 8:3, just as it is insufficient for the NRSV to say "provided for" in Mark 15:41. In both verses, the women's actions are described with the Greek verb *diakoneō*, which is a word that is most often translated as "ministering" or "serving." And neither is it clear that they are ministering *to* Jesus or the disciples, although that is a possible translation, but the grammar used there could just as easily mean that they ministered *with* Jesus and the disciples.[9]

---

7. The term from which our English term "deacon" is derived is *diakonos*, used to convey one who is in service representing a greater authority. It is not a lowly term: for instance, when Paul has lowly service in mind, he utilizes the Greek term for "slave" (*doulos*), even about himself (e.g., Rom. 1:1). In contrast, Paul uses *diakonos* and other words from the *diakon-* root to indicate Christian ministry proper, not a lesser form of service. These terms are those Jesus uses for himself when he says "the Son of Man came not to be served [*diakonēthēnai*] but to serve [*diakonēsai*], and to give his life as a ransom for many" (Matt. 20:28; Mark 10:45, NRSV; cf. John 13:1-7).

8. Matthew's Gospel may prime readers to notice women on the margins of the story, given that its opening genealogy features five surprising women (1:3, 5, 6, 16).

9. Greek is a case-based, inflected language (like Latin or German) that shows what role nouns are playing in the sentence based on their case endings. The words "him" in Mark 15:41 and "them" in Luke 8:3 are in the dative case (indirect object) and do not have any prepositions prescribing the precise directional nature of the relationship of their ministry

Whatever the English translation, it is language of generous collaboration—a response to prophetic welcome, following in the true sense of discipleship.

Finally, John's Gospel adds to our overall picture of Jesus's close relationship with female disciples in a pair of stories that never use the term "disciple" at all (11:1–44 and 12:1–8). Instead, John used terminology of *loving* to describe Jesus's connection to the sibling group of Lazarus and his two sisters, Mary and Martha (11:3, 5, 36).[10] The women did, in fact, call Jesus "the Teacher" (v. 28), which further indicates that we should understand them to have been both disciples and beloved friends of Jesus. After Lazarus's death, Jesus visited the sisters and had a profound theological conversation with Martha. She expressed trust that death was not the last word for Jesus (11:22), hope in the eschatological resurrection (v. 24), and an emphatic declaration of faith: "I believe that you are the Messiah, the Son of God, who is to come into the world" (v. 27). Jesus's intimacy with the family is on display: despite knowing that Lazarus's death would be used for God's glory (vv. 4, 15), Jesus became disturbed and wept when he spoke with the grieving sisters (vv. 33–35). The Greek text describes Jesus's emotion harshly: he was "rebuked in spirit" (the NIV softens it to "deeply moved in spirit"); and he raised Lazarus back to life.[11]

The women in Jesus's company were beloved. They served and ministered with and to Jesus. Women were entrusted as witnesses to the episodes in Jesus's life that became the heart of the Christian confession of faith: Jesus died and was raised. The women among Jesus's disciples were the first responders to these earth-shattering events. Their faith was sometimes stalwart and other times wavered (Mark 16:8; John 11:39–40; 20:13), much like the other disciples we remember and revere.[12]

---

and the indirect objects. So "ministering to," "for," or "with" could all be possible translations.

10. John uses both verbs for love that are found in the New Testament, *phileō* and *agapaō*, alternating between them in this passage: *phileō* in vv. 3 and 36, *agapaō* in v. 5.

11. In the following chapter, John recounts Mary of Bethany's anointing of her Teacher (12:3), an extravagant act that Jesus interprets as enacting prophetically the day of his burial (v. 7).

12. It is proper to give attention also to a follower of Jesus whose recognition comes from outside the Gospel texts. In Romans, Paul greets Junia, along with Andronicus, and describes them collectively as "outstanding among the apostles" (16:7). A long history of mistranslation has hampered our recognition of this woman Junia as the only woman explicitly granted the title "apostle" in the New Testament. In the last two decades, scholars

Encountering Women in Jesus's Ministry and Teaching

Beyond those who gathered to follow him, Jesus interacted with many women throughout his ministry. His engagement with women is properly understood as prophetic: that is, he is making God's welcome and extension of true fellowship in the Spirit manifest in a world that too often rejects women. The reality is that many of the women we meet in the pages of the Gospels are remembered for their actions, but their names are lost to us.

There are several stories of Jesus healing women of their physical ailments.[13] What makes the healing a prophetic act, rather than that of a physician, is that the healings often restored more than physical health. One healing that stands out—because of the severity and duration of the woman's illness, as well as the encounter itself—is that of the woman with a hemorrhage (Matt. 9:20–22; Mark 5:25–34; Luke 8:43–48). This woman, who had suffered from menstrual bleeding for twelve long years, sought out Jesus. She took the initiative and reached for Jesus—an act Jesus later named as faith.[14] Jesus listened as the woman told her story—"the whole truth" (Mark 5:33). Then Jesus called the woman "Daughter," reestablishing her full inclusion among God's people. This restoration of relationship and community status is mirrored in another encounter, when Jesus raised to life a widow's son in Nain (Luke 7:11–17). This literal life-giving restored more than the young man's life; it also restored the hopes and potential for living for his mother, the widow.[15] Her prospects for a livelihood would have

---

have tried to remedy this error. See Eldon Jay Epp, *Junia: The First Woman Apostle* (Minneapolis: Fortress Press, 2005), 23–24. In fact, Richard Bauckham suggests that this Junia of Romans 16:7 could possibly be the same woman as Joanna in Luke 8:3 and 24:10. *Gospel Women: Studies of the Named Women in the Gospels* (Grand Rapids: Eerdmans, 2002), 165–86.

13. Jesus healed many women, including the following: Peter's mother-in-law (Matt. 8:14–15; Mark 1:29–31; Luke 4:38–39); the disabled woman (Luke 13:10–17); Jairus's daughter (Matt. 9:18–19, 23–26; Mark 5:21–24, 35–43; Luke 8:40–56); Mary Magdalene, exorcised of the seven demons plaguing her (Mark 16:9; Luke 8:2); Joanna, Susanna, and many others (Luke 8:2–3).

14. It is intriguing that Jesus gives the credit for healing to the woman's faith, rather than his own power or choice (Matt. 9:22; Mark 5:34; Luke 8:48).

15. The onlookers in the funeral procession declare, "A great prophet has appeared among us . . . God has come to help his people" (7:16), likely because Jesus's healing of a son and restoration for a widow mirrors stories of two of Israel's greatest prophets: Elijah

been bleak without a husband after losing her son. Jesus healed the whole person—body, emotions, and social relationships included.

Perhaps no woman in the New Testament has been so maligned without justification as the Samaritan woman at the well (John 4).[16] After much conversation with this woman,[17] Jesus revealed that he knew she had had five husbands and, at that time, had a man who was not her husband (vv. 17–18). I have heard sermons speculating on the Samaritan woman's sordid bedroom habits, voracious sexual appetite, or gold-digging ways that Jesus supposedly exposes. Even her timing in coming to the well (noon) is said to expose her shame (vv. 6–7).[18] The trouble is, Jesus does not seem worried at all about these things that cause us palpitations. He lays no blame at the feet of the Samaritan woman for her marital history.[19] In fact, the whole point of his special knowledge about her past husbands is not to accuse her but, rather, to help her recognize Jesus's messianic identity (vv. 19–26),

and the widow of Zarephath (1 Kings 17:7–24) and two stories of Elisha—the widow's oil and the Shunammite's son (2 Kings 4:1–7, 8–37).

16. Unfortunately, there are several candidates for this "maligned without justification" distinction in Christian readings of Scripture. One, especially, is the "sinful woman" in Luke 7:37 whose sin is never specified but who is almost universally presumed by interpreters to be a prostitute. In fact, Peter uses the same adjective, "sinful" (*hamartōlos*), for himself in Luke 5:8, yet no one assumes he is confessing a life of prostitution. Jesus acknowledges the woman's sinfulness but tells a parable to indicate her forgiveness (7:40–43, 48). Then Jesus makes the woman an example of great love (7:44–47). Further, we should consider also Jesus's treatment of the woman caught in adultery, which is simultaneously gracious and direct (John 8:1–11).

17. This is the one time a Gospel author acknowledges that we should be surprised at Jesus sharing things with a woman—but, instead of this being an issue of gender, it is primarily one of ethnic identity (see v. 9).

18. This accusation in particular is entirely without historical support. The proof is in the story itself: Jesus and his disciples go to the well at this time without any reason to be ashamed.

19. Within her ancient context there are many possible reasons for a marital record like this woman's: 1) the age differences between men and women entering into marriage meant that women were frequently widowed; 2) divorce was common and lacked stigma in the Roman Empire; 3) while women could initiate divorces, they did not need to be mutual to be legal; 4) the practice of keeping concubines was not unusual; 5) most women required the support of a man based on economic necessity. See Lynn H. Cohick's well-researched consideration of these contextual issues pertaining to marriage and concubinage in the case of the Samaritan woman: *Women in the World of the Earliest Christians: Illuminating Ancient Ways of Life* (Grand Rapids: Baker, 2009), 122–28.

which seems to work (vv. 28, 39). Here, Jesus has a conversation fraught with potential landmines in terms of religious, ethnic, and gender differences. Yet Jesus refuses to be sidetracked from the main point—"I am he" (v. 26)—and trusts the woman to represent him fairly to her own people. The Samaritan woman returns to her village and so successfully evangelizes that many of them seek out Jesus, spurred on by her testimony (vv. 29, 39).

In another cross-cultural encounter, two Gospels tell us about Jesus's interactions with a gentile woman who seeks the healing of her daughter with an unclean spirit. The woman is called both "Syrophoenician" (a technical ethnic designation in Mark 7:24–30, NRSV) and a "Canaanite" (hearkening back to the gentile enemies of Israel in the Old Testament; Matt. 15:21–28). The two accounts vary, but they have in common that Jesus seemed *not* to want to help the woman's daughter, which is an uncomfortable acknowledgment for readers. Jesus's response that "it is not right to take the children's bread and toss it to the dogs" can be read either as an insult or as a test. But the woman rose to meet the challenge and answered well, turning the would-be insult into an illustration of her tenacity: even dogs can eat crumbs. She knew that Jesus was the key to her daughter's restoration, so she was ready to do whatever it took. Depending on the tone we see in this interaction, there are two ways we can understand Jesus's final response to the woman: either the woman reminded Jesus of the expansiveness of his mission and he changed his mind about healing her daughter, or the woman's answer to the question was rewarded, as Jesus had planned all along. Either way, Jesus did not become defensive but became open to compassion when faced with the woman's audacity. He accepted the woman's boldness and recognized her faith (see Matt. 15:28). Even from afar, Jesus healed the woman's daughter of her torment. Prophets are able to see God at work in unexpected places (see Luke 4:23–30).

The final aspect of Jesus's encounters with women that must be highlighted is his recognition and sharing of prophetic credit. Each Gospel tells the story of Jesus's anointing somewhat differently (see Matt. 26:6–13; Mark 14:3–9; Luke 7:36–50; John 12:1–8). Across the accounts there are differences regarding the where and who of the story. Up for grabs is even what part of Jesus was anointed (head or feet). Common to each Gospel's telling are these things: it is a woman who anoints Jesus; the perfume was expensive; when someone maligns the extravagant gift and/or its giver, Jesus comes to her defense. In Matthew, Mark, and John, Jesus invests the woman's actions with the gravity of prophecy; she is anointing him for his impending burial. When the loudest people around Jesus are angling for thrones in his kingdom (Matt. 20:21; Mark 10:35–37) or gearing up for a sword fight (Matt. 26:51; Mark 14:47; John 18:10), this woman's act drives to the heart of what Jesus sees coming: his death. For this generous act of prophetic mourning and adoration, Jesus declared that this woman was to be remembered (Matt. 26:13; Mark 14:9). Jesus instituted in advance that this unnamed woman[20] should receive honor for her fidelity and extravagant recognition of Jesus and his purpose.

When Jesus taught in parables and extended metaphors—his characteristic style—the imagery and situations were taken from everyday life. Tales of fields and their sowers, lambs and shepherds, and slaves and their masters populate the Gospels, just as they populated the ancient Mediterranean world where Jesus lived. Thus, although women were present in Jesus's parables, they were not so prominent in them as men (just as in public society in that time and place). When women did appear in Jesus's teaching, they were never the brunt of jokes or ridicule. Neither did Jesus have a subsection in the Sermon on the Mount for women only; the ideals and commands of the kingdom of heaven apply to men and women alike (Matt. 5–7).

Jesus saw fit to use typical women's work, like kneading bread, to illustrate the kingdom of God (Matt. 13:33; Luke 13:20–21). When teaching on lust, Jesus refused to blame women for the sinful desires men have toward them (Matt. 5:28). In Jesus's parable of the ten bridesmaids,[21] women exemplified the right and wrong responses (prepared and unprepared) that all humans may have toward the return of the Lord (Matt. 25:1–13). In his instruction, Jesus put forward widows—who were the lowliest among the already-less-privileged group of women—as examples of faithful tenacity in prayer (Luke 18:1–8) and generosity (Mark 12:41–44; Luke 21:1–4) for all followers.

---

20. Of course, in John it is Mary of Bethany who anoints Jesus (12:3). It is not clear whether these were two separate events or different recollections of the same occurrence. Luke's version, which focuses on the sinful state of the woman (Luke 7:39–48), is recounted much earlier in Jesus's ministry than in the other accounts and is not explicitly connected with Jesus's death.

21. This parable is also known as the parable of the wise and foolish virgins or the parable of the ten virgins. Because these young women are attendants in a bridal party, the term "virgin" is probably better rendered "bridesmaids."

Jesus highlighted his own maternal instincts in a metaphor comparing himself to a mother hen with wandering chicks (Matt. 23:37; Luke 13:34). In the parable of the lost coin, the woman who loses one of her silver coins searches for it high and low, finds it, and throws a party to celebrate (Luke 15:8–10). This woman stands, allegorically, as a representation of God! In Jesus's teaching, women were present in various ways, fulfilling different exemplary roles. In many ways, Jesus's teachings about women were in keeping with aspects of Old Testament prophetic tradition, which compared God to a mother (see Isa. 42:14; 66:13; Hosea 13:8). Jesus's teaching placed women as examples of discipleship and the kingdom, and as pointing us, through metaphor, to God.

How We Follow Jesus by Welcoming Women Today

What significance is there to Jesus's prophetic communion with women? First, we must acknowledge that a person's gender was neither a prerequisite nor a disqualifier for following Jesus persistently and well. Women were permitted and able to follow Jesus, and they did. Jesus put forward women as examples of faithfulness. Jesus entrusted women with preaching the good news of his resurrection. Women were seen as fitting parabolic analogies for all humans and—strikingly—for God, as we have seen above.

Second, Jesus's prophetic welcome establishes our community's norms. The fact is, none of the Gospels seem to apologize for or explain extensively the women's presence. If it was unusual to have women accompanying an itinerant preacher and miracle worker, the Gospels do not report that fact or reinforce the idea. In fact, one way we can follow Jesus is not to make the distinction between female and male the absolute factor in how we treat people. At times, it can be frustrating that three of our four Gospel authors tell the story of Jesus's ministry without pausing to mention that women were among the company of people following their itinerant rabbi (Luke does in 8:1–3). Naming mostly male followers might give the false impression that women were prohibited from following. On the other hand, Matthew, Mark, and John were able to tell the story of Jesus and his disciples without making a distinction between the women and men among his disciples. They refrained from distinguishing between them until Jesus reached the cross, when the women distinguished themselves by being more tenacious.[22] The prophetic witness of Jesus serves to remind Christ followers of the reality that all people—male and female alike—are spiritually enabled and, thus, equally capable of and called to discipleship.

Third, Jesus's lived-out prophecy of what God's kingdom looks like constrains us in some ways. We cannot claim that all other rabbis, Jewish men, contemporaries of Jesus, [fill in the blank] treated women like scum. Many times, arguments seek to highlight Jesus's warm welcome to women by contrasting him with his contemporaries.[23] Well-intentioned sermons and books can tend to cast all of Jesus's society, particularly Jewish culture, in a uniformly misogynistic light. Here is one example of a great book by Sarah Bessey that falls prey to this problematic logic: "During his time on earth, Jesus subverted the social norms dictating how a rabbi spoke to women, to the rich, the powerful, the housewife, the mother-in-law, the despised, the prostitute, the adulteress, the mentally ill and demon possessed, the poor. He spoke to women directly, instead of through their male-headship standards and contrary to the order of the day (and even some religious sects today)."[24] Elsewhere in the same book, Bessey states, "Everyone—including the Jews—excluded women from education, religious training, and participation (with the exception of temple prostitution in pagan worship)."[25] This statement is untrue[26] and seems designed merely to reinforce Bessey's

---

22. Apparently, the male disciples were among those who were scattered (Matt. 26:31–35, 56; Mark 14:27–31, 50–52); but compare John 19:26–27.

23. I recommend highly Amy-Jill Levine's challenging article on this point: "Second Temple Judaism, Jesus, and Women: Yeast of Eden" (*Biblical Interpretation* 2:1, 1994).

24. Sarah Bessey, *Jesus Feminist: An Invitation to Revisit the Bible's View of Women* (New York: Howard Books, 2013), 18. Do not misunderstand me: Bessey's is a lovely, thought-provoking, and gracious book. It has more things spot-on than slightly off, as is this quote. Thus, it may be unfair to use it as an example of this common but dangerous tendency, but it also illustrates my point perfectly. *Jesus Feminist* is a book I would recommend without reservation, yet it falls victim to the same overstating without evidence and stereotyping of an entire culture that many other authors, speakers, and preachers do.

25. Ibid., 65.

26. Bernadette Brooten has proven that there were women synagogue leaders in antiquity, based on archaeological findings. *Women Leaders in the Ancient Synagogue: Inscriptional Evidence and Background Issues* (Brown Judaic Studies; Scholar's Press, 1982). Amy-Jill Levine cites several pieces of literary evidence that contradict the portrayal of women as absolutely excluded from high-level involvement within Judaism ("Second Temple Judaism," 14). Further, in the multifaceted and regionally varied instances of pagan worship, there were certainly female participatory elements that did not involve

point about Jesus's positive attitude toward women, rather than serving as an actual analysis of history.[27] When, in a historical statement regarding an entire complex of societies, anyone claims that "everyone" did one thing, we should take pause. Refuting this common misinterpretation does not mean that Jesus was *not* a loving teacher who welcomed women into his company and insisted on their full personhood. As we have established, he did! But we do not do Jesus any favors by falsely accusing others without evidence. We honor Jesus by noticing, naming, studying, and emulating his treatment of women he encountered.

Jesus's welcoming of women as followers, wide-ranging healing of women,[28] teaching to women disciples, and entrusting the good news of his resurrection to women should shape our church practices today. In this chapter, we have chosen to label Jesus's friendship with, ministry alongside, teaching, healing, and treatment of women as "prophetic welcome." Christian women and men *both* have room to learn from Jesus about how to welcome women as God does. In a world that can tend to objectify or threaten women, the gathered body of Christ should exhibit welcome and safety to women. In a world that may silence or speak over women, followers of

---

temple prostitution (e.g., in Rome, the vestal virgins and Bona Dea festivals; in Greece, the female interpreter of Apollo's oracle at Delphi). On the education of Roman elite women, which varied enormously, see Emily A. Hemelrijk, *Matrona Docta: Educated Women in the Roman Élite from Cornelia to Julia Domna* (New York: Routledge, 1999). Lynn Cohick also has two chapters treating the overlapping issues of education and religious involvement for women in the ancient world in *Women in the World*, 159–224.

27. Jesus and *all* of his followers were Jewish (culturally, ethnically, religiously). Jesus gathered in synagogues for Scripture study (e.g., Luke 4:16–20), attended festivals in Jerusalem (e.g., Matt. 26:17–19; John 5:1; 6:4; 7:2–4), and followed the guidelines of the Jewish Law (so that it was only his disciples who could be accused of breaking the written and oral Torah; see Matt. 12:1–8; 15:2; Mark 2:23–28; 7:5). Jesus's disciples kept the Jewish food laws even after the resurrection and the coming of the Holy Spirit, as evidenced by Peter's response to the vision he had on the rooftop in Joppa (Acts 10:14); this indicates that Jesus had never signaled that they should do otherwise (although Mark's Gospel, upon later reflection, came to the conclusion that he did; see Mark 7:19).

28. Even among just the recorded episodes of healing women, there is a wide variety: demon possession (Mark 7:24–30; Luke 8:2); abnormal menstrual bleeding or hemorrhaging (Matt. 9:20–22, with parallels in Mark 5:25–34 and Luke 8:43–48); fever (Matt. 8:14–15, with parallels in Mark 1:30–31 and Luke 4:38–39); and even raising a girl from the dead (Matt. 9:18–19, 23–26, with parallels in Mark 5:21–24, 35–43 and Luke 8:40–42, 49–56).

Jesus should listen to and include women. The day of Pentecost ratifies this undoing of any cultural boundary markers in light of what God has done in Christ, making Christ powerfully present by the Holy Spirit (Acts 2:16–21).

Further, Jesus modeled acceptance and welcome of different ways of embodying womanhood. In the famous story of Mary and Martha from Luke 10:38–42, the conventional interpretation is that Mary's choice to sit and listen to Jesus was right, while Martha's attempt to carry out many tasks of ministry and/or service[29] was wrong, or lesser. The NIV, NRSV, and CEB all translate verse 42 using the word "better." The Good News Translation goes so far as to say that "Mary has chosen the right thing." And we often read Martha and Mary as pitted against each other, where only the "better" one can emerge victorious.[30] But the Greek text says that Mary has chosen "the good part."[31] Jesus said that only one thing is necessary, and he affirmed Mary's choice to listen as a disciple: that was *the good part* (*tēn agathēn merida*). Yet he never said that Martha's choice to busily minister was wrong or bad. The only comparison Jesus made was between Martha's *many* things troubling her (v. 41) and the *one* thing that was truly necessary (v. 42). Among her many things Martha could still choose to focus on the one vital thing: Jesus. What a difference it makes to imagine that it is not a competition between Mary and Martha. What freedom we sense when our translations refrain from seeking a "better" between the two women and simply affirm that Mary has chosen well and that Martha was free to do the same.

It is vital to acknowledge that Martha was also doing what was unquestionably valued as "good" in a communal society that puts utmost honor in hospitality.[32] Ancient readers likely *could not* have seen this passage as a rejection of Martha; her active hospitality honored Jesus and would not have

---

29. The terms used of Martha in 10:40 are *diakoneō* (verb; "to serve, to minister") and *diakonia* (noun; "service, ministry").

30. See an example of this comparative reading in Bessey's *Jesus Feminist*: "Jesus defended [Mary's] right to learn as his disciple; he honored her choice as the better one" (19).

31. The NASB, ESV, and KJV translate the phrase more accurately in this case.

32. This reading of the unquestioned value of hospitality in communal, honor/shame cultures was driven home for me by Dr. Alice Yafeh. See her article for a fuller exploration of this interpretation in light of her home-cultural context: "The Liberative Power of Silent Agency: Reading Mary (Luke 10:38-42) through the Eyes of Cameroonian Rural Women" in *Postcolonial Perspectives* in *African Biblical Interpretations*. Eds. Musa Dube, Andrew Mbuvi, Dora Mbuwayesango (Society of Biblical Literature, 2013), 408–17.

needed to be affirmed as a good thing. Yet Jesus refused to shame Mary—as may have been culturally customary, and as Martha perhaps wanted him to do. Martha was the one who compared their actions (v. 40). Martha may have bought into the tense situation created by her own cultural scripts that enforced one best way to exist as a woman. But Jesus did not accept those restrictive scripts. He simply affirmed that Mary's choice was good. There was room for Mary and Martha both; there was opportunity for Martha to change her perspective. Binary thinking makes us want to name Mary the winner of this competition and to boot Martha into the loser category. Yet this is *our* inclination as modern readers; it is not Jesus's in the narrative itself. The lesson that there was room for both women to be themselves and to respond to Jesus speaks prophetically to us today.

Finally, there is a related issue that requires some careful reflection, coming from another angle at the question of Jesus and women today. Here, I am not asking how Jesus treats women as a resource for how we should do the same. Instead, I want us to consider how Jesus's prophetic work can and does shape our imaginations. Jesus's own embodiment and his particularity mean that Jesus is male. Yet, as Savior and Lord to men *and* women, we are to follow Jesus's example regardless of our own gender identities. This desire for Christlikeness is good and part of the Spirit's work in our sanctification. The trouble is, Jesus's prophetic attributes and characteristics that we desire to emulate can be applied unevenly to men and women, based on gender expectations, in ways that are harmful and unholy.

For example, I find myself occasionally in groups that consist primarily of women ministers. This community is nearly always edifying, encouraging, prayerful, and inspiring. Occasionally, however, the desire to follow Jesus's example is selective, skewing Jesus's prophetic voice and actions problematically. I will provide just two examples. A female seminary student might express frustration at being passed over for a ministry position, despite her qualifications and sense of fit. The problematic response chimes in: "Jesus did not need a position or acclaim in order to do ministry. Why should you?" Suddenly, expectations of compensation and a sustainable living wage to help provide for a family are made to seem selfish in light of Jesus's ministry.[33]

---

33. Jesus's ministry is exemplary for our own—vocational and otherwise—in many ways, but its duration and sustainability cannot be one of those. Based on the Gospel witnesses, the longest Jesus's ministry is thought to have lasted is three years. Even Paul, whose own

Or, a woman might voice a struggle or hurt she has experienced in ministry and receive a response along these lines: "You need to get over it. Jesus didn't push back or protest when he was mistreated. And he died on the cross for us. What do you have to complain about?" Jesus's willing suffering and death are held up as a rationale for women to persist silently in pain and mistreatment. This attitude also dismisses the church community's accountability to act as faithful witnesses to Jesus's prophetic vision.

On one hand, looking to Jesus's model of self-giving has validity. Indeed, Jesus calls his disciples to take up their crosses and follow him (Matt. 16:24; Mark 8:34; Luke 9:23). Self-emptying love—often called by its Greek terminology, *kenosis* (see "emptied" in Phil. 2:7, NRSV)—is a central, Christlike pattern of giving oneself away for the sake of others. Yet this portrait of Jesus is lopsided on its own. In Scripture Jesus is, indeed, portrayed as humble, meek, gentle, and willing to suffer. However, he is *also* portrayed as an extraordinarily charismatic speaker (Luke 4:32; John 11:47–48); as a confrontational debate partner (Matt. 22:23–33; John 8:39–59); as willing to spark conflict to drive home a point (Mark 2:1–12); as ready to rebuke untruth, even with close friends (Mark 8:33; Luke 9:51–56); as avoiding death at many junctures prior to crucifixion (Luke 4:29–30; John 7:1–9; 8:59); as unconcerned with breaking social conventions (Matt. 12:46–50; Luke 5:27–32; John 4:27); as unafraid to direct his despair and disappointment to God (Mark 15:34); as committed to taking time alone (Mark 6:45–47; Luke 5:16); as not pressured by others' sense of urgency in ministry (Mark 1:35–39); as downright angry at injustice and spiritual abuses (Matt. 23; Mark 7:9–13; Luke 9:45–46; John 2:13–22), and, sometimes, as angry simply because he was hungry (Mark 11:12–14, 20–21).[34]

When only one side of this complex portrait of Jesus our Lord is held up as the model—and particularly applied when women are perceived to need correction and restraint—we have a serious problem. This same, meek-Jesus logic has been used for great ill: to require women to stay with abusive

---

self-sacrificial ministry catalyzed dynamic growth of the early churches in gentile regions, seems to have accepted support from many of the churches he planted (Phil. 4:10–20), although not from others (2 Cor. 11:7–9).

34. My students call this "hangry Jesus." (*Hangry* is slang for anger or irritability arising from hunger.)

partners,[35] to justify women needing to be the ones to give up their callings to unquestioningly defer to their spouse's pursuits, as evidence for the necessity of ragged and "selfless" exhaustion as the portrait of true motherhood, and to manipulate victims into silently enduring rape and sexual assault by authority figures. This meek-Jesus is not the real, living, and particular Jesus but, rather, a figment of our wishful and destructive imaginations.

Now, the converse is also true: that is, if we manipulate aspects of Jesus's life and actions as our excuse to be rude, divisive, and condemning (e.g., "Get behind me, Satan!" from Mark 8:33), we likewise are ignoring the Jesus of excessive forgiveness (Matt. 18:22), of turning the other cheek (Matt. 5:38–42), and of reconciliation (John 21:15–19). If, as it seems to me, this unbalanced meek-Jesus tends again and again to be applied to women, and seldom or never to men, there is a problem. I have observed a discomfort with women expressing negative emotion or asserting their place of value in the community following Jesus. Even seeking an outlet to express aloud frustration for mistreatment can be seen as too demanding or un-Christlike. But the prophetic work of Jesus invites women to follow him in insisting that the church is not faithfully the community of God's people without the welcome of women. Quite often, prophets must remind the people to be faithful, using voices that are not at all meek. This prophetic activity flies in the face of a popular Christian culture that imposes an impossible standard of self-negating meek-Jesus—often by women—on themselves or upon other women. This self-negating standard is a recipe for burnout, for the renewed life we have in Christ being traded in for emptiness and exhaustion.

Women's inclusion at all levels of ministry is directly in line with Jesus's own prophetic work and ministry. As the church, we need to notice and be self-critical of the expectations we have of women—and Christian women, especially. Do we allow a breadth of expressions of femininity, as Jesus did? Are we receptive to the prophetic voice if it comes to us in a woman's voice? Or do we uphold the unbiblical view that there is only one right occupation or attitude of femininity (whether consciously or unconsciously)? Likewise,

---

35. A powerful blog post by Gary Thomas addresses this issue and gives anecdotal evidence to this phenomenon: "Dear Church: It's Time to Stop Enabling Abusive Men," *For Every Mom*, https://foreverymom.com/marriage/enough-enough-church-stop-enabling-abusive-men-gary-thomas/.

do we impose impossible standards on women—ones we dare not ask of men—and close off prophetic possibilities that could prod us toward further faithfulness in exchange for a bankrupt and unbalanced portrait of Christ?

Women, are you living a selfless, empty, self-negating life and believing a false gospel that this is your way of following Jesus? If so, reject that lie. Follow Jesus the prophet, who embodies a vision of God's kingdom in which your own prophetic voice finds its proper place. Receive the love of God. Embrace the full, multifaceted and real portrait of Jesus, which permits you to speak out prophetically against sinful abuses. See the prophetic work of Jesus as it welcomes you as a daughter of God; follow his prophetic instruction when a welcome is withheld from you (Matt. 10:14). Dive into introspection and repentance without permitting shame to take hold. Dream big, kingdom-shaped dreams in keeping with Jesus's prophetic imagination. Allow space for learning and preparation, for rest and the experience of true Sabbath. Seek out healing and rich relationships and receive the good things others will pour into you. Then, you may pour out and expend that love on others, not wringing out the last, meager drops from a parched towel but lavishly, like Christ, from a deep reservoir of grace.

Suggestions for Further Reading

Bauckham, Richard. *Gospel Women: Studies of the Named Women in the Gospels.* Grand Rapids: Eerdmans, 2002.

Bessey, Sarah. *Jesus Feminist: An Invitation to Revisit the Bible's View of Women.* New York: Howard Books, 2013.

Burden, Suzanne, Carla Sunberg, and Jamie Wright. *Reclaiming Eve: The Identity and Calling of Women in the Kingdom of God.* Kansas City: Nazarene Publishing House, 2014.

Cohick, Lynn H. *Women in the World of the Earliest Christians: Illuminating Ancient Ways of Life.* Grand Rapids: Baker, 2009.

Leach, Tara Beth. *Emboldened: A Vision for Empowering Women in Ministry.* Downers Grove, IL: IVP Books, 2017.

Miller, Susan. *Women in Mark's Gospel.* Journal for the Study of the New Testament Supplement Series 259. New York: T&T Clark, 2004.

5 ✝ FOLLOWING JESUS AS PRIEST

Amy Peeler

ALTHOUGH it is common for many Christian believers today to speak about Jesus as our High Priest, what exactly do we mean when we say such a thing? Historically, where does this idea come from? In what way does Jesus fulfill and redefine the office of priest? Could our understanding of Jesus as a priest actually shape and aid the way we follow him? As commonplace as it may be for his followers to consider Jesus a priest, it is a fairly minor theme in the New Testament, which contains only a handful of references to Jesus in this office. Of course, impact is not always weighed by word count. Though Jesus is not *called* a priest very often, the whole of the New Testament presents him as the mediator—the representative—between God and humanity. Mediator is, of course, a priestly role, yet Jesus inhabits it uniquely because he is both God and human.

The writers of the New Testament and the earliest followers of Jesus lived in a place, time, and culture in which priests functioned as an everyday part of life. Because of the ubiquity of priestly ministry in the Greco-Roman world, early readers would readily identify and find great meaning in his priestly role. If we are going to gain a deeper understanding of what it means to understand Jesus as a priest, we need a historical sketch of priesthood in the first century to provide a context for us. That historical context will then prepare us to investigate biblical texts that portray Jesus as a priest. We will see that these passages suggest that Jesus mediates between the human and the divine, as do other priests. As he does so, however, he is superior to any other priest because he is God, and he also humbles himself more than any other priest because he offers his own body as the sacrifice.

Historical Background

If we are going to understand how the New Testament recognizes the priestly ministry of Christ, we must understand the cultures of the authors and readers, which include the pervasive Greco-Roman[1] culture as well as the Jewish religious background. Together, both of these influences shaped the way first-century people understood what a priest was. Ultimately, understanding these influences helps us understand how they would have considered Jesus a priest.

The practices of the Jewish priesthood are embedded, unsurprisingly, in the narratives and instructions of Israel's scriptures. The first priest in the Hebrew Bible is Melchizedek, priest of the Most High God and king of Salem, whom Abraham meets after his return from the battle of the kings (Gen. 14:17–20). Melchizedek performs several actions that come to be codified as the work of priests. He blesses Abraham, receives a tithe from him, and gives him bread and wine. Not until the book of Exodus, however, does the law of Israel offer specific instructions for the priests. Some are mentioned when the people first meet God before Mount Sinai (Exod. 19:22), but then Exodus 28–29 describe their vocation in detail. They are set apart by the tribe from which they come, the clothes they wear, and the rituals performed both upon them and by them. In their distinct role, they can help to interpret the will of God for the future, and assist judges in discerning the best decision for quarreling people.

Because religious practices and life are so tightly interwoven, as the priests teach about the holiness of God in the sacrifice, they are teaching

---

1. The term "Greco-Roman" refers to the culture of ancient Greeks and Romans. Culturally, a Greek sensibility (mythology, religious practices, philosophies, rhetoric, drama) was infused throughout the ancient world from the regions of Western Europe to North Africa to Persia and beyond. Even though it could be considered watered down by geographical distance, the adoption of Greek culture—which we call *Hellenization*—happened through centuries of trade and contact. Greek culture was further politically incentivized with the military conquests of Alexander the Great (336–323 BCE) and the Macedonian/Greek generals he left to rule after his death—which they did for 200 to 300 years. Although the Roman Empire is historically subsequent, it inherited and purposely imitated much of Greek thought. Thus, a term like "Greco-Roman" serves to identify the broader cultural milieu in which many local, indigenous cultures also operated. Even while regions retained differences, Greek was the language of trade and politics and Greco-Roman culture the common broth in which these areas were steeped in the centuries prior to and following Jesus's life.

about much of the Torah (Lev. 10:10–11; Deut. 33:10), disclosing what is clean and unclean, holy and common.[2] Then they help draw the boundaries around God's holy place and communicate God's blessings when people visit. Chiefly, they are the stewards of the place on earth where God's presence dwells, and they facilitate the prayers and the sacrifices of the people. Much of Leviticus describes the specific sacrifices they offer to God on behalf of the people of Israel. These can be for sins committed but also for thanksgiving, peace, and cleanliness.

In subsequent eras of Israel's history, the actions of the priest continued as long as a place of worship stood,[3] but the office became entangled in the shifting political tides. Antiochus Epiphanes intervened in the selection of the high priest based on whoever provided the most substantial bribe.[4] When the Maccabees revolted against Greek control and put in their own brother as high priest, Jonathan may have been committed to the cause of purity, but he did not come from the previously established, high priestly family. The office of priest suffered turmoil again with later wars against Hasmonean families during the time of the Herods (37 BCE–CE 34). By the first century, the high priest performed the roles of priesthood under the control of Rome. By the time Jesus entered the scene, many Jews might have been looking for a priest who would serve God faithfully without being tainted by politics.

---

2. T. Desmond Alexander and David W. Baker, eds., "Priests, Priesthood," *Dictionary of the Old Testament Pentateuch: A Compendium of Contemporary Biblical Scholarship* (Downers Grove, IL: InterVarsity Press, 2003), 650.

3. The temple Jesus knew is referred to as the Second Temple because the first Jewish temple, Solomon's Temple, was destroyed by the Babylonians in 587/586 BCE. The temple was rebuilt after Judean exiles returned from Babylonian captivity (circa 516 BCE), and it was greatly reconstructed, enlarged, and improved by Herod the Great (though not completed until long after Herod's death). This Second Temple was destroyed down to its foundations by the Romans in CE 70.

4. Antiochus IV Epiphanes was the ruler of one of the Hellenistic dynasties from 175 to 164 BCE. As the king of the Seleucid Empire in Syria (not to be confused with the modern state but comprising the area that today is known as Turkey and beyond), the empire north of—and at times in control of—Israel in the Hellenistic Period. He was the archnemesis of everything the Jewish people valued, as told in the books of 1 and 2 Maccabees (found in the Old Testament Apocrypha). His heavy-handed forcing of Greek culture and religion on his subjects in Jerusalem and the surrounding Jewish-populated areas generated the Hasmonean revolt, the uprising led by a family of priestly father and brothers nicknamed the Maccabees.

Priesthood and sacrifice were not just Jewish phenomena, however. Many early readers of the New Testament, whatever their ethnic background, would also have been familiar with priests in the Greco-Roman world. In Greco-Roman life, priests were advisors on religion. They assisted with festivals and directed individuals, groups, and the country on religious matters. Priest was a position of honor and, in some cases, much power, but it was not limited to one ethnic subgroup (like the Levites for the Jewish people), nor was it always a lifetime position. Similar to the Jewish Levites, however, they also assisted with or presided over animal or blood sacrifices to the gods.

A priest in the first century, then, was an honored servant of God (or the gods) who facilitated a relationship with the divine through instruction and enactment, frequently through sacrifice of produce or, more often, animals. When early converts to Christianity heard Jesus described as a priest, anyone in any region of the Mediterranean world would have a conception with which to compare Jesus's priesthood. Given the ubiquitous presence and important role of priests throughout the Mediterranean world of the first century, it is actually surprising that, in the New Testament, only the book of Hebrews explicitly reflects upon Jesus's leadership of his people in a priestly manner.

John 17

Though Hebrews is the only book of the New Testament to refer directly to Jesus using priestly terminology, John's Gospel contains many fascinating themes that inform the way we understand Jesus as a priest. Although many Bible editions include a section heading titled "The High Priestly Prayer," John 17 does not explicitly name Jesus as priest—but it does communicate Jesus's role as mediator: Jesus communicated a message from God the Father to humanity and prayed on behalf of humanity to God. Yet in John's Gospel, Jesus's mediator role is rather lopsided, with heavy emphasis from the God side of the equation. A priest was meant to present sacrifices and prayers to God from other humans and then pronounce forgiveness from God. But Jesus demonstrated a different kind of priesthood, in which he gave gifts to humanity from God and continued to ask God for blessings to bestow on his people. Humans are ever the beneficiaries in this prayer. While people could react to God's gifts, they never had to request them through Jesus. He did that all on their behalf.

In this prayer, Jesus recalled the great gifts he had already brought to humanity in the act of tabernacling among them.[5] As frequently mentioned in John, Jesus gave eternal life (17:2) because he revealed the name of the eternal God (vv. 6 and 26), and the communication continued as he disclosed to them the words God gave to him (vv. 8 and 14). When they heard these words, they had great joy (v. 13). Finally, Jesus acknowledged that he shared God's glory (v. 22), thereby making them aware of God's love for them, which is the same love the Father has for his Son (v. 23).

Jesus then most clearly demonstrated his priestly acts when he prayed on behalf of humanity. Acknowledging that his hour of departure from the world was at hand, Jesus prayed for those he would leave behind, that they might be kept in the name the Father and Son share (v. 11). He returned to the same theme a few verses later, when he asked that God the Father keep them from the evil one (v. 15). Their being in the world left them in a precarious position for which they needed divine sustaining power. Second, Jesus prayed that these followers, and those who would become believers because of their testimony, would become unified (vv. 11, 21, 22, 23). This unity was meant to be the same unity the Father and Son share. He asked that they all be brought into a relationship of the inexplicably intimate unity of distinct persons.

Therefore, Jesus described two relationships of paralleled unity: his and the Father's, and those who believed in him. He then prayed that the two groups would come together; that the believers might be with him so they can see his glory (v. 24). He desired that the love the Father shared with him would be given to his followers and that he would be among them (v. 26). If this prayer was granted, he could not be with them the same way he had been, since he was to depart from the world. Nevertheless, his presence—as other sections of John indicate—would remain among them through the gift of the Spirit. Jesus, the one who is sanctified, would be with them, and his presence is connected to his prayer that the Father would also sanctify his people in the truth (v. 17). For the words he gave them already are truth.

The claims John highlights in the words of Jesus are quite amazing. Jesus affirmed that he shared and has always shared the same glory, name,

---

5. The word in John 1:14 for "dwelt" or "dwelling" is *skēnaō*, related to the word for tent, *skēnē*, used to describe the tabernacle where the priests worked.

and love of God Almighty. John describes a relationship of mutual giving and equal glory between the Father and the Son, which means that, in this prayer recorded in John 17, God himself intercedes to pray for humanity. Moreover, in the same kind of giving movement, Jesus asked that the Father grant humanity a share in their glory, love, and unity. Jesus, like other priests, prayed to God on behalf of humanity, but he prayed *as God* and asked for that which only God could decide to and be able to grant—unified life now and, in the future, unity in the divine life of God.

Hebrews

As the only book that directly calls Jesus a priest, Hebrews discusses Jesus's priesthood explicitly and extensively. Hebrews recognizes without question that Jesus is superior to other priests, but the author does not completely devalue other priests. Instead of priesthood being a bad thing that Jesus *replaces*, the perspective found in Hebrews presents a priest's calling and service as good things that Jesus *replicates* and—because of who he is—at which he excels. Therefore, the author presents numerous similarities that Jesus shares with other priests.

The first similarity between Jesus and other priests, and one that might seem painfully obvious, is that priests should be humans. The humanity of Jesus is not an inconsequential point in Hebrews or in any other book of the New Testament. The author states that all priests are taken from among humankind (5:1), and by that stage in his argument, he has already spoken with great clarity and complexity of Jesus's full and real human experience (2:5–18), which is one side of his mediator role. Since priests go between humans and God, Jesus as a priest must be able to understand the human condition. Therefore, the author explicitly says that he has experienced suffering and temptation so that he can sympathize with those who experience the same (2:17–18; 4:15).

As a human priest, Jesus's position serves to point toward God. Jesus has become a merciful and faithful high priest with regard to the things aimed toward God (2:17). One cannot adopt this role flippantly or even out of a personal desire. A priest must be called by God. Aaron and his descendants were, and so was Jesus. The author has scriptural support for that assertion, quoting Psalm 110 as a text spoken by God to Jesus: "You are a priest forever" (Ps. 110:4; Heb. 5:6).

In his role as priest, Jesus performs actions that are similar to other priests. He is part of a covenant system, a relationship set up by God with his people in which blood sacrifice deals with the problem of sin that corrupts and separates. Jesus offers that sacrifice in a tabernacle (Heb. 10:19–21). In addition to sacrifice, Jesus prays for the people in his care (7:25). The author of Hebrews understands the ministry of Jesus—on earth, on the cross, and in heaven—through the lens of priesthood. He looks to the model laid out in Israel's scriptures, and the priestly practices with which his audience would be familiar, to understand and articulate the Son's saving work.

While Jesus shares all these things with other priests, he is unlike any other priest in vital ways. His unique status features prominently in the very first section of the sermon in Hebrews. There, along with the assertion that Jesus has made purification for sins (1:3), the author also proclaims the confession his audience shares that Jesus is the Son of God, which makes him King (1:8) and sovereign over God's house (3:6), God's creation (2:8–9), and God's enemies (1:13). It becomes clear that his Sonship does affirm his royal status, as it did for the kings of Israel (Pss. 2; 89; 2 Sam. 7), but that is not all. He is the Son of God in such a way that he shares in God's name, God's worship, God's creating, and God's eternality. It was unusual in Israel's ideals for one person to embody the roles of both king *and* priest; it is, therefore, *unique* to claim that this High Priest is at the same time the Son of God in a way unlike any other (Heb. 4:14; 5:5; 7:28).

This divine identity shapes his priesthood into one without parallel—a priest unlike anything the world has known before—because divinity has chosen to interact with humans in an embodied way. The author of Hebrews goes on to state that Jesus did not exist as a priest forever in time past. Instead, this was a vocation to which he was called to take up as he became incarnate (5:5; 10:5–8). Hence, while other priests simply exist as human and experience their priestly call, the Son willingly *chose* to be human. Sent by God the Father (an *apostolos*, 3:1), Jesus came into the world proclaiming his intention to take up a body and to do God's will (10:5–9). Just as the Father spoke his relationship as Son,[6] so also God called him to be a priest (5:5).

---

6. It is affirmed in Christian tradition, as expressed in Hebrews and also the Gospel of John, that the relationship of Father and Son existed before the foundation of the world. See also the Nicene Creed.

As the author of Hebrews has affirmed the priesthood of Jesus as a call from God (Ps. 110:4), he also realizes he has a major exegetical problem on his hands. Jesus, as he and his readers know, comes from the tribe of Judah (Heb. 7:14), and the law given by God to Moses does not designate members of the tribe of Judah to serve as priests but only those from the tribe of Levi (Exod. 28–29; Lev. 8, 21–22; Num. 1:47–54). This seeming discrepancy may very well explain why other books of the New Testament eschew this title for Jesus. The author of Hebrews—so committed to the divine conversation of Psalm 110, as well as the theological power of this way of interpreting the work of Christ—must therefore show that he is qualified on other grounds.

In Hebrews, we see that Jesus was not a priest called through the line of Aaron and the Levites but into the order of Melchizedek, that mysterious, first priest-king who met Abraham in Genesis 14. In Jesus's human life, when he was preparing for his role as priest in this line, he experienced suffering and temptation, which made him able to be merciful and sympathetic to those he serves. Commentators wonder whether the author of Hebrews poses a difference in empathy between Jesus and other priests. While human priests merely control their anger against those who are ignorant and deceived (Heb. 5:2), Jesus is fully sympathetic. Though he experiences the gamut of human temptations, he remains perfectly without sin (4:15) so that he never has to offer a sacrifice on his own behalf (5:3).

He does not offer a sacrifice for himself; instead, he offers *himself*, something no other priest ever did. They could not do so because sacrifices were to be without blemish, so their weaknesses would disqualify them. Jesus, however, as one who was without sin, holy, without evil, and undefiled (7:26), offered himself, his body, and his blood as the means of atonement (9:14). The author of Hebrews, in a move of great creativity[7] that profoundly shaped Christian theology, connects Jesus the Messiah's shameful death on a cross (12:2; 13:12–13) and his bodily resurrection (13:20) to his priestly offering. He takes himself—a perfect, sinless offering—to the heavenly tabernacle (4:14–15) where God the Father dwells to make one sacrifice for sins sufficient forever (10:15–18). Once this work is completed, he takes a

---

7. This is possibly in conversation with brief comments by Paul in Romans 3:21–26, in which Jesus is referred to as a "sacrifice of atonement" (v. 25).

seat at the right hand of God because he has fully dealt with the problem of sin and separation.

His priesthood, however, does not end with that one offering; the sacrifice only inaugurates it. In fact, God has said that Jesus will be a priest forever (Ps. 110:4; Heb. 5:6). Now that he has defeated death (Heb. 2:14–15), he will live forever, embodied as the God-Human Priest-King. He now is the mediator of the new covenant by which God and God's people, with clean hearts, can be in relationship forever (7:22; 8:8–13; 9:15; 10:14–18; 12:24). He lives forever to make intercession for those who are following him (7:25). He is the author and finisher of faith, so that those who are obeying and following him may reach the goal of dwelling in God's presence forever (12:1–2). Jesus follows the pattern of priesthood because of *who he is*: the Son of God who willingly became a son of humanity. His priesthood in its preparation, inauguration, and continuation supersedes all other priestly work. Humanity needs no one else to mediate between themselves and God.

Conclusion

Jesus's priesthood, in its heights and in its depths, can never be superseded. His divinity and his compassion leave humanity with no need for any other mediator, for God has mediated and restored the relationship severed by sin and death. The common priestly role of leadership, discernment, and sacrifice prepared the early Christians to understand the awesome uniqueness of Jesus's prayers for them and his sacrifice on their behalf. It is a good thing to know what kind of priest Jesus is and what a powerful role that played in the first century, but such historical and biblical knowledge only prepares us to follow him. We still need to know *how* to follow him.

First, knowing what kind of priest Jesus is should elicit from us mighty praise. We can hardly grasp the fact that the God of the universe—not some demigod or lesser being but God's very self—came to restore the divine-human relationship. This truth gives us the correct framework for gratitude regarding our salvation. We are to wonder at and praise God for the complete degree to which God took on the human condition. This is a kind of praise that necessitates self-knowledge and honesty. We recognize better God's gift of knowing us when we are already acquainted with ourselves and with our shortcomings. We can be honest because, as Hebrews instructs, we know that, in Christ, God will be sympathetic to our condition. When we follow

Jesus as priest, we praise him as a priest living into the completeness of his role, praising him in his divinity and thanking him for his humanity.

Second, Jesus's incomparable priesthood offers comfort and instruction for those who serve in Christian leadership. We toss around a common phrase that Christians should "be Jesus to people." And, while emulating and representing the character of Christ is the ideal for which we strive, Christians—and especially those in leadership—need to cautiously avoid developing a Messiah complex. When Christian leaders follow Jesus as priest, they know that Christ alone is the great High Priest; we do not have to fill those shoes. There is still a need for human leaders—even Hebrews recognizes this need (13:7, 17)—but the role of a leader is to facilitate everyone's movement toward Jesus and to deepen their relationship with God.

To follow Jesus as priest is to know that what God has done on our behalf is beyond what any human priest could do. Jesus became human, lived perfectly, died as a sacrifice for the sins of all, and conquered death. This priestly, divine-human mediator continues to work on our behalf: the Son sympathetically listens to our prayers and provides intercession for us, that we might be kept by him until we dwell in the love of the triune God forever.

6 ✝ FOLLOWING JESUS THE CRUCIFIED

Diane Leclerc

The Priestly Mediation of the Cross

If the main theme of Christ as priest is found in his action as mediator throughout his life, then the cross is the consummate and unparalleled symbol of his mediating work. The role of mediator manifests itself in two parallel, priestly functions. The first is to represent humanity to God. This, of course, is the primary function of earthly priests, whether speaking of Jewish history or even the contemporary office of priest or pastor today. As humans, pastors can take the needs of the people before the throne of grace. It is, thus, extremely important to confess the full humanity of Jesus in his priestly role. Jesus is able to fully experience and empathize with every aspect of human life, including death. Certainly the resurrection enables him to continue the role of advocate before God presently. But, ultimately, Jesus's full humanity enables him to identify fully with us and represent us to God.

The second priestly function is Christ's ability to represent God to us. Unlike earthly priests, Jesus is fully divine and therefore completely capable of communicating the heart of God to humanity. Indeed, "In the beginning was the Word [*logos*], and the Word [*logos*] was with God, and the Word [*logos*] was God" (John 1:1). It is extremely important for the Gospel writer to stress that Jesus was not just **a** *logos* (which is Greek for "word, message, logic") similar to the Greek notion of *logos* as an emanation of God but less than divine.[1] Rather, in John's Gospel, **the** *Logos* is none other

---

1. The term "emanation" comes from the Latin, meaning "to flow from." Within Greco-Roman philosophical thought is the concept that all secondary things *flow from* (i.e.,

than God, who takes on flesh and dwells among us. Key in the Council of Nicaea is that only Jesus as God can save humanity.[2] The perfect human, or even a demigod, cannot save. Only one who shares the divine *ousios*—a Greek term meaning "the very essence"—can extend salvation rightly to those who cannot save themselves.

This brings us to the atonement—that is, the idea that Christ's death on the cross brings salvation. Interestingly, there is no single theory that is considered the orthodox position regarding *how* Jesus brings salvation through the cross. No individual theory dominates the biblical witness.[3] Unlike Christology, which was "settled" in the early church period through various ecumenical councils that produced creeds, atonement theology has never been settled in the same way. The continuing development of various theories throughout the history of the church bears out that there is no single, correct interpretation of relevant biblical passages. However, most Christians hold to a one-correct-interpretation model in practice. Many Christians believe they know what the Bible says about the atonement, but the fact is, they are depending on extrabiblical sources from the early church, the medieval period, the Reformation, and beyond. Most Christians are not aware that there are so many options but are only aware of what is most emphasized in their own church tradition.

---

emanate from) a primary force/deity. (This Greek concept influences many later religious movements.) That is, the primary source emanates from itself beings of related but lesser quality, which in turn emanate things of descending power/goodness (perpetually). *Logos*, in this sense, emanates from God and, although divine, is less divine and pure than its source, which is precisely the sense of *logos* that John explicitly rejects in 1:1.

2. The Council of Nicaea gathered in CE 325 for the purpose of developing a coherent understanding of what would become some of the Christian tradition's most distinctive beliefs. Chief among them was the relationship between Christ's divine and human natures, and the implications that relationship had for human salvation.

3. The forthcoming discussion will expound on these, but as a brief introduction, several examples of atonement theories and their biblical support include: ransom/*Christus Victor* theory—that Christ rescues people held captive by sin or Satan (e.g., Matt. 20:28); moral influence theory—that the love of God expressed in Jesus's death on the cross exemplifies love and motivates us to follow Jesus's example (e.g., 1 John 3:16); satisfaction theory—that the debt of our sin required a sacrifice to God and that Jesus acts as the perfect sacrifice to repay what is owed to God (e.g., Heb. 10:14); penal substitution theory—that God needed to punish sinners to maintain God's honor and justice and that Jesus takes the Father's punishment in place/on behalf/instead of sinful humans (e.g., Isa. 53:5; Gal. 3:13).

The types of atonement theories generally fall into two categories: objective and subjective. I would argue that each category is an expression of an overemphasis on one side of Christ's priestly mediation at the neglect of the other. For instance, there are theories that see the primary need in salvation as appeasing God, which we have called satisfaction theories of the atonement. While it is true that only one who can fully advocate for humanity must be divine (for only the divine can enter into the divine space to make such a plea), nevertheless, the overemphasis within the satisfaction view is on the humanity of Jesus. Satisfaction theories put it this way: *Jesus, the human one, took our place by being punished on our behalf. Once so punished, he can take a satisfactory sacrifice before God as a form of payment. In response, God's wrath or God's honor is satisfied or appeased, and humans can be forgiven.* As demonstrated, objective theories are out of balance by giving excessive prominence to Jesus's identification with humanity, temporarily setting aside Jesus's divinity.

In the more subjective theories of the atonement (for example, moral influence theory), the "audience," if you will, shifts. The cross becomes the greatest expression of God's love for us, *to* us. The mediatory overemphasis here is on the representation of the divine to humans. Subjective atonement theories express: *God seeks to communicate, through the life and crucifixion of God's Son, the lengths to which God will go to offer us reconciliation.* God does not have to be appeased in order to be just. The word "appease" (from the satisfaction theory) shifts to the word "appeal." The cross is God making an appeal to humanity. Appeal is not to be understood in some juridical sense, as an appeal in a courtroom but as an appeal to the heart of a beloved. God appeals to humans—through the divine mediator, Jesus—that love can conquer sin.

It becomes clear why certain traditions focus on certain theories: what one believes about the nature of God determines what one believes about the efficacy of the cross. Is God essentially sovereign? Is God essentially love? The objective and subjective theories line up under what we believe most about God. Of course, convictions about the essential nature of God spill into every systematic category, but perhaps none so essential as soteriology.[4] The traditional emphasis seems clear enough, no matter the

---

4. It could be argued that the theory of *Christus Victor* bypasses the objective-subjective dichotomy and therefore better represents a balanced view of Christ's priestly mediation.

objectivity or subjectivity of the theory: God forgives sinners. All theories introduce the cross of Jesus Christ as pivotal in God's saving act. The cross is absolutely priestly. All theories see the cross as symbolizing God's reconciling act in Jesus.

It seems obvious to say that the cross is symbolic—since it has been used as a symbol for two thousand years. Here, however, we are emphasizing it as symbolic of Christ's priestly mediation. We must remember that, in Christian thought, a *symbol* has a particular meaning. A symbol participates in the reality to which it points. A symbol stands in as a type of shorthand for more elaborate sets of meaning. Another characteristic of a symbol is that it opens levels of reality that are otherwise closed—a reality that cannot be reached in any other way. "In the creative work of art," as Paul Tillich presents as an example, "we encounter reality in a dimension which is closed for us without such works."[5] The cross as a symbol participates in all that was accomplished there. And it opens us to a deeper dimension of spiritual reality.

For Christians, the cross has traditionally symbolized the means of salvation. It is an ironic and paradoxical symbol, in that it points to life out of death, healing out of suffering, victory out of defeat—to name a few. But what the cross symbolizes precisely can also depend on what atonement theory one embraces. For some, it is the greatest symbol of God's love and God's compelling appeal to humanity. For others, it symbolizes the appeasement of God's wrath. Whether it is portrayed as *morally influencing* or *satisfying*, the cross's symbolism has been limited to dealing with the guilt and salvation of the sinner. However, the cross, as a potent symbol of Christ's priestly mediation, is pregnant with possibility for symbolizing salvation for the *sinned-against*.

Andrew Sung Park rightly notes that Christian theology has a long history of analyzing the doctrine of sin—or hamartiology—from the perspective of the sinner only.[6] As such, the problem of sin and the promise of salvation emphasize the importance of the confession of sin—the prayer

---

Sin is the target in the sights of this theory. The divine human is the one who overcomes the power of sin.

5. Paul Tillich, *Dynamics of Faith* (New York: HarperCollins, 2001), 48–49.

6. Andrew Sung Park, *The Wounded Heart of God: The Asian Concept of Han and the Christian Doctrine of Sin* (Nashville: Abingdon Press, 1993).

of repentance to God, reconciliation with God, justification by faith in God, and sanctification in God. The need of the sinner is perceived as a strictly vertical need. Yet there has been little analysis and discussion of the oppressed—the victims of those same (now saved) sinners.[7] While the doctrine of sin, following Augustine and Luther, is most often expressed as some form of a self curved in upon itself, as pride and self-centeredness,[8] Park seriously questions to what extent the doctrine of salvation itself can be myopically and ironically self-centered on behalf of a powerful oppressor—if salvation here is primarily about him or her being let off the hook. Too often there is a unilateral perspective in atonement theology that neglects the power of the atonement for those who suffer because they have been sinned against.

The *sinned-against* are victims of violence, abuse, and various forms of oppression who come in all shapes and sizes. Victims are of various ethnicities, young and old, male and female. There are no identifying features on which to base our proclivity to categorize, other than common horrible experiences. Yet victims too stand in need of salvation—as healing, redemption, and liberation—often desperately. Certainly, some are literally held captive and need to be freed, like victims of sex trade and human trafficking. Others' captivity is more psychological, even spiritual. All victims need liberation in some way, in the sense of being freed from a disempowering and de-humanizing wounded-ness, which may be presently happening or that happened years earlier. All need the liberation of being re-humanized and re-dignified. This is no less a need for salvation than those who seek forgiveness. The sinned-against also need to be freed from their burden. Unlike sinners, however, it is not a burden of their own making but one imposed on them by others.

The common biblical question "what must I do to be saved?" cannot afford to linger in the realm of eternal destiny that concerns itself only with the

---

7. Ibid., 72–73.

8. I, and others, have challenged the dominant theological stance that equates sin with pride. Catherine Keller writes, "Feminist theology has shown . . . that the traditional definitions of sin as pride, arrogance, self-interest, and other forms of exaggerated self-esteem *miss the mark* in the case of women, who in this culture suffer from too little self-esteem, indeed too little self." *From a Broken Web: Separation, Sexism, and Self* (Boston: Beacon Press, 1986), 40. See also Diane Leclerc, *Singleness of Heart: Gender, Sin, and Holiness in Historical Perspective* (Lanham, MD: Scarecrow Press, 2001).

propitiation of the sinner's sin and the offer of future reward. It is a question that must be answered in the literal, where literal salvation is often its chief command and its initiating gruesome circumstance is painfully real and present. The meaning of the words "what must I do to be saved?" is radically different from different mouths. From the sinner: how can I escape the eternal consequences of my sin? From the sinned-against: how will I survive this present, existential horror of deep, lingering, and open wounds?

It is crucial to realize that, to address the needs of victims, we do not have to find another salvation narrative. The cross retains potent capacity as a strong metaphor for the sinned-against. Yet the narrative of the cross and of Christ's priestly mediation needs to be told differently. The symbolism is there; it needs to be "brought to bear" (up under) the victimized. The symbolism for the victimized extends Christ's priestly role.

The Cross as Priestly Symbol for the Sinned-Against

If we look at the cross from its backside—as salvific for the victimized—themes do emerge. Namely, the cross of Jesus Christ is symbolic of 1) violence and scapegoating; 2) nakedness and shame; and 3) abuse and abandonment. The goal of this analysis is to open up new dimensions of reality and to open up the "hidden depths of our own being."[9] We are not creating the symbol; rather, we are bringing into the light what has been in the shadows.

Violence and Scapegoating

The cross is a symbol of violence. Jesus endured unspeakable violence that started with his scourging (e.g., Mark 15:16–20). The flagellation of Christ is seen more vividly in liturgy and art than in the Gospels themselves. The scene has been depicted in art for centuries. Most paintings depict a violent, angry, and obviously painful scene, some wrought with graphic blood and wounds. Films such as *The Passion of the Christ* (2004) burn horrific images into the minds of viewers, as Jesus's back becomes a gaping mass of bloody flesh and exposed muscles and sinews. In Jewish law, flogging was limited to a maximum of forty lashes, but the Romans had no such limitation for non-citizens. It is probable that Jesus succumbed to shock from a copious amount of blood loss.

---

9. Tillich, *Dynamics of Faith*, 49.

Liturgically, the flogging of Christ is one of the Stations of the Cross, memorialized on Good Friday. After the scourging, which could be seen as Pilate's intent for full punishment—before being pushed toward crucifixion and the Barabbas debacle[10]—Jesus began the journey toward his death. The suffering continued. He walked, attempting to carry the load wood on his de-fleshed back, until someone else had to take over and pick up the cross. At Golgotha, the violence escalated. His hands and feet were nailed. His muscles and sinews tore under the weight. His crown bled. He suffocated slowly. He refused analgesic. He died an excruciating death.

In the background, in the shadows, we see hidden people look on with keen perception of the pain, for they are familiar with its visceral reality. They truly understand. They are the child huddling in the closet, praying their father will not come tonight to do unspeakable, truly violent and violating things to them. They are the woman in the mirror trying to cover the bruises with makeup, to no avail. We see an Asian young woman running naked down a back road in Vietnam. We see a man instantly incinerated by nuclear fire in Hiroshima. We see skeletal people waiting their turn for the gas-chamber showers at Auschwitz. We see beaten children, rape victims, dismembered and neglected bodies of veterans, the elderly who die alone in rank conditions, slaves of all kinds, the diseased, the desperate, and the despised. We see people—intermingled yet solitary—who tentatively and slowly move toward the front, toward the foot of the cross, and quietly beckon, "Speak to *me!*"

Jesus was killed violently. He understands violence that affects body and soul—bone-chilling, bone-cracking, flesh-tearing, heartbreaking violence. He indeed has something to say to these sinned-against victims. He is not limited by the isolating and confining helplessness of pain, though he experienced it to the core of his being. He comes with priestly care and whispers, "By my stripes you are healed."

Nakedness and Shame

The cross is a symbol of nakedness and shame. The full weight of this symbol can be difficult for modern, Western readers to access. More recent scholarship has shown how deeply embedded an honor-shame system was

---

10. See Matt. 27:15–26; Mark 15:6–15; John 18:38–40.

in early Christian culture. Alicia Batten provides an introduction to the discussion:

> The cultural values of honor and shame figure centrally in various New Testament texts' articulation of Christology. It is widely agreed that crucifixion was one, if not the most dishonorable form of execution within the Roman Empire. It was a horrible death and perceived as such by Greco-Romans and Jews. The victim would be stripped naked and publicly put to death. This public dimension of the death was especially humiliating. Thus the New Testament authors faced the challenge of the fact of the crucifixion and its dishonorable nature. In the Gospel of Mark, for example, Jesus is abandoned by his disciples, tortured and strung up on a cross, where he cries out to God. Mark does not belabor Jesus' suffering, but he does not hide it either. The element of dishonor that Jesus has suffered is in fact a central element of Mark's overall Christology. Here, the Christ is the suffering Son of God, degraded and bereft. In a sense, Mark grants a certain honor to something that most ancients would find repulsive. Mark redefines, in many ways, what it means to be a Messiah or Christ. The true Messiah is a humiliated, tortured figure. Such an idea must have been quite difficult for many ancient people to comprehend or even want to consider.[11]

Much of Christianity has followed Mark's lead in making the humiliation of Christ honorable. But in doing so, over time, we have divorced ourselves from the immensity of the original shame. Christianity has lost the radical nature of the faith of the people who embraced such a disgraced Christ figure.[12] And it has certainly forgotten the level of dishonor and degradation such people faced themselves. To put on the sufferings of Christ may or may not have entailed their own physical suffering, but what is sure is that they faced the societal shame of following after such a socially appalling Savior.

What is missed now, as a result, is the sense that Jesus Christ fully empathizes with those who are covered in shame, and particularly with those

---

11. Alicia J. Batten, "Honor and Shame in the New Testament," *Bible Odyssey*, http://bibleodyssey.org/tools/ask-a-scholar/honor-and-shame-in-the-new-testament.

12. Paul's discussion in 1 Cor. 1:18–31 illustrates this radical perspective well. He took for granted that a death by crucifixion was shameful (to claim otherwise was utter foolishness) yet reinvested this obvious shame with divine honor for those who associated themselves with Christ.

whose shame is no fault of their own but has been imposed upon them by guilty others (a common effect, especially, of sexual abuse). If we make the cross only a symbol of triumph, we leave the shamed hovering in the shadows at the backside of the cross. It is theologizing that (appropriately) transfigures the cross from death to life, from sin to holiness, from hate to love, from weakness to power, and from shame to honor. However, at face value, in its historical context, the cross was a symbol of all that was repulsive.[13] Only our post-crucifixion culture—where the symbol of shame eventually lost its power—can glamorize a cross around one's neck, fixed with gold and diamonds. Yet victims often view themselves as repulsive, unacceptable, even ugly. The abused cannot see their pain reflected in the glorified and exalted cross. The message that Jesus endured the cross, experienced its utter humiliation, and died exposed and naked can communicate to victims that Jesus understands innocent shame.

Jesus bled innocent blood. In Leviticus 16:6–10 there is a sacrificial provision in which the blame for persons' sins was symbolically placed on a goat, which was then sent out away from the people. The word "scapegoat" has made its way into cultural and religious images. A scapegoat is a person who is unfairly blamed for something others have done. Thus, scapegoats are innocent and do not deserve the punishment that should be assigned to the guilty. Jesus functions as a symbolic scapegoat who vicariously steps in and bears the guilt of the world by enduring and absorbing the violence of the cross. Yet, as such, he is also fully able to empathize with victims who are also scapegoated, also innocent of any guilt for the crimes against them. There is no anguish like the injustice of bearing the shame that belongs to another. Like Jesus, victims bear a shame and pay a penalty that is not their own. Jesus, as scapegoat, absorbs the shame of the world and can lift it from the maimed shoulders of the innocent.

Abuse and Abandonment

The cross is a symbol of abuse and abandonment. Jesus suffered at the hands of the soldiers, who followed the orders of the powerful leaders of Rome and Jerusalem. To state the obvious, he was clearly abused physically. He was victimized, suffering violence at the hands of others. But this must be

---

13. Imagine the cross as analogous to an implement of institutional execution that is more familiar to us today: a hangman's noose or an electric chair.

said delicately because, theologically, it is crucial to understand that Jesus embraced the cross voluntarily. In the garden of Gethsemane, Jesus could have said no to God, but his ultimate response was willingness: "yet not my will, but yours be done" (Luke 22:42). We have to maintain this truth or else risk falling into the dangers of monophysitism, where Christ's temptations are no longer real because they are eclipsed by a strictly divine nature.[14] It is essential to maintain his free-will choice to allow himself to die.

Yet it is also vital to say that the cross was not merely suicide, without perpetrators. There were persons involved in the whole Passion narrative, who stand guilty—directly or indirectly—of Jesus's death.[15] A traitor killed him when Judas gave him up for a bag of silver (Matt. 26:14–16). A group of self-righteous, religious men killed him when the Sanhedrin—the rulers of his own people—found him guilty of blasphemy (Matt. 26:59, 65). A crowd killed him when they chose Barabbas over Jesus (Luke 23:18–25). A Roman governor killed him when Pilate washed his hands of the whole matter (Matt. 27:24). A few soldiers killed him when they pounded the nails and threw lots for his clothes (John 19:24). His own disciples either fled or passively watched him die (Matt. 26:56), and Peter denied him outright (Mark 14:66–72).

Jesus was clearly physically abused, but we can only speculate about the level of his emotional or psychological trauma. Although Jesus was finally victorious as he cried out, "It is finished" (John 19:30), there are other moments on the way to the cross (such as the garden), and on the cross itself, where we see the emotional strain in addition to the physical. The emotional strain is most acutely seen in his cry, "'Eloi, eloi, lema sabachthani?' (which means 'My God, my God, why have you forsaken me?')" (Mark 15:34). Not only have human beings denied, whipped, tortured, deserted, and killed him, but God as Godself has abandoned the Son. It has been a theological conundrum to try to decipher what occurs in the Trinitarian

---

14. Monophysitism is a position—rejected by most of the early church—that maintains only one nature in Jesus. (In Greek, *monos* means "one" and *physis* means "nature.") In a well-known iteration of this heresy known as Eutychianism, the human and divine natures collide in Jesus, and the divine nature overcomes the human. The problem is that, in doing away with Jesus's divine nature, Jesus would not have identified with the nature of humanity, including humanity's ability to suffer.

15. The references that follow in this sequence are selective; many more could be cited. These are presented to provide a starting point for deeper scriptural study.

Godhead as Jesus Christ dies on the cross. Some have suggested it is crucial to affirm that the whole Trinity died and that there was no essential separation; to others, it has been imperative to say that God turned God's back on the Son, truly abandoning him to die and thus fracturing the essential Trinity. What matters here is Jesus's existential experience of God's abandonment, which increases the depth of his empathy with us.

One option for dealing with God's abandonment of humanity comes in the form of protest theology, also known as Jewish protest theology or Holocaust theology. In its most popular form, it is expressed by persons such as Elie Wiesel in books like *Night*.[16] Protest theology focuses on the existential experience of God's abandonment and is open to the possibility of God's guilt. Allowing persons to feel abandoned by God is key; they should not be argued out of it. Yet the idea of the atonement for the sinned-against, from a Christian perspective, parts ways with Holocaust protest theology. That is, God's appeasement to the abandoned is ultimately maintained *precisely* as Jesus, who is God, experiences God-forsakenness. Jesus was a victim of God in the experience of being abandoned. At the center of this type of atonement theology, or what I call backside theology, is Christ's cry of agony: "My God, my God, why have you forsaken me?" Backside theology permits us to protest against God for allowing the atrocities of victimization. Again, these protests must not be short-circuited, or even short-lived existentially. Theoretically, they take us to an interesting insight about the atonement.

While objective theories of the atonement focus on God's need to be appeased, and subjective theories focus on God's appeal to humanity's need for redeeming love, atonement directed toward the sinned-against is indeed God's appeal *and* appeasement toward them.[17] The wounded and broken need the infinite and healing love of God. But, standing bloodied by the injustices of others, the sinned-against also need some satisfaction. To push it even further, in traditional objective theories, Christ stands in our

---

16. Elie Wiesel was born in Hungary, survived the Holocaust, immigrated to the U.S., and died in 2016. He became a prolific author, describing and reflecting on the suffering of his people in Nazi concentration camps. He was a respected voice for Holocaust survivors. Wiesel's writing asks theological questions and refuses to accept answers provided by theodicy (put simply, theodicy is the question of why bad things happen to good people, if God is good). His first book, *Night*, was published in French in 1955. There are numerous English editions available today.

17. This view echoes aspects of 2 Corinthians 5:16–21.

place as substitutionary sacrifice to appease God's sense of justice. Rather, for victims, who similarly stand in need of justice, Christ's victimization could be seen as in God's place, as God's appeasement directed toward the sinned-against. This would constitute a grand reversal of objective theories that atone for sinners. I am not suggesting that this appeasement parallels the payment motif found in objective theories. God is not giving Jesus as payment to victims to compensate for their suffering. But if we can define appeasement in this instance as God's compassionate acknowledgment of the injustices endured by victims—as an indirect result of creating the potential for evil in the beginning, and allowing for suffering in the pres- ent—injustice, in a sense, is atoned for. This does not wipe away, cure, or dismiss the suffering. But God's all-encompassing understanding of the agony of victimization offers a type of solidarity that only a crucified God can offer. It gives a wider meaning to the reality that Jesus bore sin: it is a priestly bearing.

What we know of God's nature matters here, especially as revealed in Christ. If we are to allow for appeasement in this sense, the fundamental question is, is there a place infinite enough in the loving heart of God where there is a willingness not only to forgive but to be forgiven? Not only to appeal but to appease? Is there a place where God takes sin into Godself, a place where God has blood on God's hands, a place where God experi- ences God's own abandonment? Christians have abandoned themselves to the cross as our only hope. Ultimately the cross will fail us or save us all. Sinner and sinned-against hope in faith that God will save, explicitly through the kenotic act of the crucified one.

As mediation to victims in particular, the cross represents Jesus the Christ's deep solidarity as he allows himself to be victimized. Jesus hangs with us on the hook of innocent blame; there, we experience an intimate presence. But also, in Jesus's bearing of guilt, God hangs on the hook as well, willingly; God takes blame upon Godself. Divine love so infinite that it al- lows us a chance to forgive even God. And so, even if we remain in the pain that still lingers in shadows of the cross, and even if we still feel entombed by our circumstances, we can even now participate, if ever so hopefully, in the power of our own resurrection when God will save us to the uttermost and wipe away our tears. None of this is possible without our Priest.

What Are We to Do?

We move now to ask what it means to follow Jesus the crucified priest. Jesus states clearly that, if we seek to be his disciples, we must take up our cross (see Luke 9:23–24). These verses are extremely familiar to many of us, especially those of us in my own holiness tradition, who believe that consecration and surrender are key to the Christian life. Yet, while we can be experts at denying ourselves, we have not always understood the call to pick up our crosses. We have interpreted it to mean that we have a cross to carry from time to time, maybe an illness to bear or some period of personal struggle. In light of our focus on the sinned-against in this chapter, it is extremely important to resist the temptation to say they are bearing crosses. This is where the orthodox proclamation that Jesus's sacrifice was volitional is key. Enduring something that happens to us against our will is not "taking up our cross." Cross-bearing is a deliberate, intentional, and conscious choice, and it also serves a purpose.

Christ died on behalf of others as a means of rescue. We take up our crosses when we suffer on behalf of others. The purpose of cross-bearing is to love others. Sharing in the sufferings of Christ explicitly means embracing the lengths to which love goes. Taking up a cross cannot be associated with victimization for the very reason that the suffering of victims is senseless—it has no purpose. Cross-bearing lives out the (secondary) purpose of our existence: to love our neighbors as we love ourselves. Following the crucified Christ, therefore, calls us to priesthood, as in the priesthood of all believers. When we live out our priestly function toward those who suffer, it matters from whence we come.

Henri Nouwen has popularized the concept of a "wounded healer."[18] He writes profoundly on this point: that God's grace and love work through us most strongly not out of our wholeness but out of our brokenness; not out of our soundness but out of our wounds; not out of our strength but out of our weakness. God does not *cause* us to be victimized. Suffering of a certain magnitude is truly absurd and meaningless. But the redeeming God, in the aftermath, can use our wounds as a source of comfort and even healing in the life of another. As we have seen from Jesus himself on

---

18. Henri J. M. Nouwen, *The Wounded Healer: Ministry in a Contemporary Society* (New York: Doubleday, 1972).

the cross, we must not underestimate the priestly power of true empathy. There is healing in the simple but profound words, "I understand." When we do this, the blood from Christ's wounds mingles with the blood from our wounds, which mingles with the blood of their wounds. And in this, we usher them into the very presence of Christ. It is not accidental that this image can be understood eucharistically as well as practically. Consequently, yet not insignificantly, such redemption extends to us as our wounds are recycled in the economy of God.

For those of us who wish to take up our cross on behalf of and in solidarity with others but who have not significantly suffered ourselves (although we all suffer from life to various degrees), we should not underestimate the priestly potential of presence. Stanley Hauerwas wrote a book that explores the issues surrounding the problem of evil without being seduced by the typical and inadequate answers of theodicy—God, Medicine, and Suffering. What makes the book so compelling is his use of narrative (both fictional and real life) to come at inexplicable suffering. He strongly suggests that the experience of isolation is profound in the face of grief and pain. He weaves several stories together, all involving the death of children. In his conclusion he arranges, to great effect, a series of quotes from Nicholas Wolterstorff's Lament for a Son. Wolterstorff is a Christian whose grief does not cause him to question the existence of God, although "he expresses surprise that the elements of the gospel—particularly the hope of resurrection—he thought 'would console did not.'"[19]

Wolterstorff writes, "Eric is gone, here and now he is gone; now I cannot talk with him, now I cannot see him, now I cannot hug him, now I cannot hear of his plans for the future. That is my sorrow."[20] Then Hauerwas concludes his book by reminding the reader that there are no truly satisfying answers to the problem of evil. He ends with the following:

Just as Wolterstorff is not interested in false or easy answers, so he is not interested in false or easy comfort. So do not tell Wolterstorff that death—the death of Eric—is "not really so bad. Because it is. Death is awful, demonic. If you think your task as comforter is to tell me that really, all things considered, it's not so bad, you do not sit with me in my

19. Stanley Hauerwas, God, Medicine, and Suffering (Grand Rapids: Eerdmans, 1990), 149.

20. Nicholas Wolterstorff, Lament for a Son (Grand Rapids: Eerdmans, 1987), 31.

grief, but place yourself off in the distance away from me. Over there, you are of no help. What I need to hear from you is that you recognize how painful it is. I need to hear from you that you are with me in my desperation. To comfort me, you have to come close. Come sit beside me on my mourning bench."[21]

As representatives of humanity, and as representatives of Christ to those who suffer, priestly presence is that to which we are called. In this sense, we take up our cross when we carry the crosses that others bear. And we hold them, and hold for them Christian hope, even if silently. We hold for them a hope in the future resurrection, when God will save us to the uttermost and wipe away our tears. Our Priest calls us as priests to cry with others in the meantime.

---

21. Hauerwas, *God, Medicine, and Suffering*, 151; Hauerwas quotes Wolterstorff, *Lament for a Son*, 34.

7 ✟ FOLLOWING JESUS THE RECONCILER

Dick O. Eugenio

"IN CHRIST," the apostle Paul wrote, "God was reconciling the world to himself, not counting their trespasses against them" (2 Cor. 5:19, NRSV). This profound statement of salvation points to an aspect of Jesus's work that we can consider priestly in function, offering to us the beautiful possibility of living as reconciled to God and to one another. This priestly reconciliation that Jesus offers also carries a challenge of stewardship: once Jesus has offered us the possibility of a reconciled life, we are also entrusted with "the message of reconciliation," making us Christ's "ambassadors" to others of the hope of being reconciled (2 Cor. 5:19–20).

The Reconciling Priest

Reconciliation basically refers to the re-union of two or more parties who were previously alienated from or hostile toward each other. It comes from the Latin word *reconciliare*, which means "to conciliate."[1] It refers to the restoration of that which was once enjoyed but has been lost. Reconciliation happens when "enmity is changed to friendship" and when there is a

---

1. The Greek terms that we translate as "reconciliation" or "reconciling" are *katallagē* and *katallassō*, respectively. In the three verses of 2 Cor. 5:18–20, there are five words from the *katall* stem. Our English term reflects the Latin equivalent, *reconciliare*. The Greek verb *katallassō* has the main meaning of "change" or "exchange" but is used in situations of reconciliation to demonstrate a positive change in a relationship.

change of relationship from "hostility to hospitality."[2] In Colossians 1:21–22, as Paul expressed beautifully, reconciliation happens when active opposition to God is transformed, by Christ, to friendship. By our resistance to God, we were alienated from God and were actually God's enemies, but, through Christ, we are reconciled to God.[3] No human action can restore our broken relationship with God. The re-union of the alienated is the work of God through Christ.

John Wesley expressed the reconciling work of Christ in terms of mediation. In his commentary on Matthew 1:16, he wrote that "we are by nature at a distance from God, alienated from him, and incapable of a free access to him. Hence, we want a mediator, an intercessor, in a word, a Christ, in his priestly office."[4] Several things may be pointed out from this short quotation. First, because of sin, the human condition is that of alienation (Col. 1:21). "The wages of sin is death" (Rom. 6:23), and humanity has no self-cure to this predicament. Second, Christ "himself is our peace, who has made the two groups one and has destroyed the barrier, the dividing wall of hostility" (Eph. 2:14). Jesus is the sole mediator between God and humanity (1 Tim. 2:5). For Wesley, Jesus accomplishes his reconciling work as a priest, mediating the relationship between humans and God, restoring what we humans broke.[5]

Of course, Jesus does this work by standing within a long line of priests who came before him. The primary role of priests, according to the Old

---

2. Ferdinand Nwaigbo, "Christ Jesus: Our Peace and Reconciliation," *African Ecclesial Review* 51–52 (December 2009–March 2010), 364.

3. In contrast to the conditional reconciliation that is prevalent in Jewish thinking, the reconciliation that God effects with and for humanity is by absolute grace. See Svetlana Khobnya, "Reconciliation Must Prevail: A Fresh Look at 2 Corinthians 5:14–6:2," *European Journal of Theology* 25 (2016), 129–30.

4. *Wesley's Notes on the New Testament*, vol. 1, *Matthew to Acts* (Kansas City: Beacon Hill Press of Kansas City, 1981).

5. See also John Wesley's sermon "The Law Established through Faith II," where he attributes the work of reconciliation "to God by blood" particularly to the "great High Priest," in *The Works of John Wesley*, vol. 2, *Sermons II*, ed. Albert C. Outler (Bicentennial Edition; Nashville: Abingdon, 1985), 37. The relationship between reconciliation and the priestly office of Jesus Christ, found in Wesley, is helpful and foundational for this chapter, but to strictly compartmentalize the three offices of Christ—prophet, priest, king—and to appropriate salvific works specific to each office does not do justice to the holistic nature of the work of Christ. Jesus's reconciling work is not limited to his priestly office.

Testament, is to act as mediators between God and humanity. The Jewish sacrificial system was essentially meant as the avenue of forgiveness and reconciliation with God, and the Levitical priesthood was specifically instituted so the people of God might receive assistance in the temple when they offered their sacrifices. A priest has an exalted position among the people because he is one "through whom and through whose ministry people draw near to God."[6] The work of Jesus the priest has many dimensions, but here, we are primarily interested in his reconciling work. How does the priestly Christ reconcile the world to God? What actions of his are specifically noticeable as reconciling works? Jesus is the Reconciler, not just the worker *of* reconciliation. How, then, do we follow, imitate, and reflect him? How do we participate in his ministry of reconciliation?

One of Us and with Us

It is important for us to realize that Jesus reconciles the world to God through himself. Reconciliation is not just the work that Jesus does outside himself, like a detached potter making clay pots. Rather, the work of reconciliation is embodied in him — it *is* who he is. Jesus is not just the one who *made* peace for us (Col. 1:20), as if peace were some kind of artifact or trinket; he himself *is* our peace (Eph. 2:14). Jesus is not a temporary instrument through whom God accomplishes his purposes but is a priest in his own being.[7] In short, the entire earthly life of Christ is his priestly existence.

The first place we find the priestly mediation of Jesus is in his act of becoming flesh—the incarnation. The affirmation "God became human" is rich with salvation implications. The breach of relationship between God and humanity is so complete that "a new form of mediation" is required to deal with the situation. In the words of Colin Gunton, "It

---

6. David J. MacLeod, "Christ, the Believer's High Priest: An Exposition of Hebrews 7:26–28," *Bibliotheca Sacra* 162 (2005), 331. Ultimately, Jesus is the High Priest prefigured in the entire Levitical priesthood. Based on the terms of the covenant, Jesus is not qualified to be priest because he is from the tribe of Judah, not Levi (Heb. 7:14). Nevertheless, he is a priest in the order of Melchizedek (Heb. 5:6). In fact, the book of Hebrews extols Jesus as *the* High Priest.

7. Using the two categories of priesthood set forth by Deborah W. Rooke, we can understand that Jesus is not merely a functional priest but also an ontological priest, in "Jesus as Royal Priest: Reflections on the Interpretation of the Melchizedek Tradition in Heb. 7," *Biblica* 81 (January 2000), 81–82.

requires that the one through whom God created the world is now media-tor of reconciliation."[8] Mediation of reconciliation is precisely what Jesus accomplished in his life. His birth is the miraculous and unprecedented union between God and humanity. God descended to us so that, through Jesus, we might ascend to the Father in communion. This mediation was what Paul referred to as "the grace of our Lord Jesus Christ, that though he was rich, yet for your sake he became poor, so that you through his poverty might become rich" (2 Cor. 8:9). The God-human union is a reconciling union. In the words of Ferdinand Nwaigbo, "Jesus Christ in his person and work established reconciliation between God and the human race. Jesus Christ as a true man and true God takes the position of the sinful human-ity, justifying it through his own life, death and resurrection, and carrying it through to its goal."[9]

Jesus's priestly reconciliation is his redemptive solidarity with sinful humanity. Interestingly, Jesus's being one of us is an important element of his priesthood: "Therefore he had to become like his brothers and sisters in every respect, so that he might be a merciful and faithful high priest in the service of God, to make a sacrifice of atonement for the sins of the people" (Heb. 2:17, NRSV). Jesus is our eldest brother, by virtue of our being children of God in particular (John 1:12; Rom. 8:14–17; Gal. 3:26; 4:6–7), and because Jesus is the firstborn in general (Rom. 8:29; Col. 1:15, 18; Heb. 1:6; Rev. 1:5). As one who experienced all of humanity's weakness, Jesus—our brother and priest—is able to empathize with us (Heb. 4:14–15). Patrick Gray calls this Jesus's "fraternal empathy" with us.[10] But Jesus is not only one of us; he is also with us. Jesus's other name, *Immanuel*—"God with us"—is a statement of reconciliation. In Christ, God dwells with and among God's enemies in holiness and love. He comes to dine with sinners. He calls tax collectors to be his disciples. He touches the unclean. Throughout his earthly ministry, Jesus shatters the walls that alienate sinful humanity from the holy God. Jesus was reconciling the world to God by being with the people.

---

8. Colin Gunton, "One Mediator: The Man Jesus Christ: Reconciliation, Mediation and Life in Community," *Pro Ecclesia* 11 (2002), 149.

9. Nwaigbo, "Christ Jesus," 363.

10. Patrick Gray, "Brotherly Love and the High Priest Christology of Hebrews," *Journal of Biblical Literature* 122 (2003), 335.

Of course, the incarnation of the Son is unique and unrepeatable. Following, imitating, and reflecting who Jesus is does not entail any sort of becoming divine for us. However, the lessons on solidarity, fraternity, and empathy are important. Reconciliation is only achievable when we actively reach out to the different other, or to our complete opposite (nonbelievers and even Christianity bashers). However, we do not reach out superficially, like organizing sporadic medical-mission trips in order to satisfy our consciences. Jesus dwelt among the people: he entered their homes and stayed with them. He was one of us and one with us. The way we follow, imitate, and reflect Jesus in this way is commonly described as *incarnational ministry*. The examples of David Brainerd among American Indians, Mother Teresa among the poor of Calcutta, and Toyohiko Kagawa among the labor unions of Japan come to mind prominently. They exemplify for us what it means to truly follow Jesus's priestly and incarnational work of reconciliation. We are called to spend less time in peace-talking conferences and more time in actual peace-making activity in our communities if we hope to follow the priest who reconciles with those who are unlike him. Steve Murrell captures this sentiment well: "We are irrelevant to our sinful generation because we spend too much time around Christians and not enough time around the unchurched."[11] Very few actually spend time with the poor and the unreached. We need to learn how to make the presence of God felt in the lives of people by being present with them ourselves.

Moreover, following Jesus means acting in embodied, flesh-and-blood ways. Jesus is the Reconciler. He is the Way, the Truth, and the Life. Jesus's teachings were not mere words; he embodied them and exemplified them in life. We embody peace and reconciliation through our unity and love for one another as a church. Whether we care to admit it, our divisions in the church are the mightiest hindrances to our ministry of reconciliation. Following Jesus is not only following his ministry of reconciliation; it is also following his pattern of life reconciled to the Father and to the world. To be a priest of reconciliation means living at peace with everyone, which requires patience, kindness, gentleness, goodness, and love. We embody reconciliation by being reconciled and reconciling. This requires us to be understanding of one another's weaknesses, forgiving of one another's

11. Steve Murrell, *WikiChurch: Making Discipleship Engaging, Empowering, and Viral* (Lake Mary, FL: Charisma House, 2011), 97.

offenses, and embracing of one another's differences. We can be priests of reconciliation like Jesus by having his character, his compassion, and his mindset (Phil. 2:5–8).

On Behalf of Us and for Us

Our ability to act as priests and agents of reconciliation is a gift that is given to us and that comes—at Jesus's own expense—as a result of being reconciled to God. We must consider, then, the stunning and beautiful reality of what it means for Jesus to be the priest who offers reconciliation by making himself the sacrifice that reconciles. While his entire life demonstrates this characteristic, the cross has a special place in Jesus's priestly work of reconciliation. As R. J. McKelvey asserts, Jesus's passion is "in its entirety a priestly prayer."[12] There is no doubt that the crucifixion is the act of Jesus the High Priest performing the sacrifice of at-one-ment between God and humanity. He established peace through his blood (Col. 1:20). The alienated "have been brought near by the blood of Christ" (Eph. 2:13) on the cross, where he "extinguished their hostility" (Eph. 2:16, BSB).

The beauty (and horror) of Jesus's crucifixion is that, as priest, he was both the sacrificer and the sacrifice. In the Old Testament, one cannot speak of sacrifice without priest or priest without sacrifice. The group of priests known as the Levites was specially called to offer sacrifices on behalf of the people. The priesthood of Jesus, however, is unique because the sacrifice he offered to the Father was his own life. Jesus is "a new kind of priest."[13] Scripture provides a wealth of images for this priestly identity: Jesus offers himself as a guilt offering (Isa. 53:10), an offering of sin (Rom. 8:3), sin for us (2 Cor. 5:21), and a ransom for many (Matt. 20:28). He was the lamb slaughtered for the people (Exod. 12; Isa. 52:13–53:12; John 1:29, 36). He laid down his life (John 10:11, 17–18) for the scattered children of God (John 11:51–52). He did all of this *on our behalf* and *for* us. The high priest Caiaphas providently affirmed this truth when he said, "It is better for you that one man die for the people than that the whole nation perish" (John 11:50). Jesus was the "one

---

12. R. J. McKelvey, *Pioneer and Priest: Jesus Christ in the Epistle to the Hebrews* (Eugene, OR: Pickwick Publications, 2013), 68.
13. Nicholas G. Piotrowski and David S. Schrock, "'You Can Make Me Clean': The Matthean Jesus as Priest and the Biblical-Theological Results," *Criswell Theological Review* 14 (Fall 2016), 13.

---

man" who died for all people. In the words of David MacLeod, "Jesus took to himself this one destiny of all human beings . . . He died as a sacrifice in the place of sinners, and that once-for-all act is all that is needed to provide forgiveness forever."[14] Consequently, those who are forgiven of their sins through Christ have peace with God (Rom. 5:1–2) and are able to approach him with confidence (Heb. 4:16).

The drama of reconciliation on the cross is very profound, especially when we realize that, on the cross, Jesus was undoing the sins of Adam and Eve that led to our alienation from God. We remember that Adam and Eve hid from God behind trees when they sinned (Gen. 3:7–10). They were ashamed. They realized that they were naked, and they did not want to be exposed to their own Maker. They were also afraid that God would punish them. So they hid. The once harmonious relationship between God and humanity was ruined by sin. Jesus Christ, however, undid all of this on the cross. We must realize that Jesus, bearing the sins of the world upon himself (1 Pet. 2:24), was lifted up on a tree, completely naked and exposed to God. He presented himself in the position of a sinner to the Father—naked and shamed—so that humanity might no longer feel ashamed before God. He bore the punishment of sin—death—upon himself because humanity is both afraid and unable to bear it. The naked human Christ on the tree confesses before the Father and accepts the punishment of sin on behalf of and for all humanity. Jesus the High Priest is the self-sacrificing *mesites*—the one who goes between—who establishes reconciliation between God and sinful humanity by becoming a sacrifice himself (Heb. 8:6; 9:15; 12:24).[15] Or, as Paul put it, "God made him who had no sin to be sin for us, so that in him we might become the righteousness of God" (2 Cor. 5:21).

---

14. MacLeod, "Christ, the Believer's High Priest," 343; Teresa Okure, "'The Ministry of Reconciliation' (2 Cor. 5:14–21): Paul's Key to the Problem of 'the Other' in Corinth," *Mission Studies* 23 (2006), 113.

15. Gray, "Brotherly Love," 345–46. According to Gray, the *mesites* is the elder brother (Heb. 2:10–18; 12:5–11) who acts as the pacifier between the father and the siblings. He diverts the judgment of his father—from his brothers to himself—and lifts up the sibling who feels inferior or ashamed.

Following the Reconciler

What does it mean, then, for us to follow Jesus Christ? Jesus portrays that the way of reconciliation is the way of suffering and death for the sake and on behalf of others. There is no other way if we are to follow Jesus. Colin Gunton reminds us: "The cost of the mediation of salvation by the man Jesus Christ was a life of constant trial and temptation, ending with the supreme gift of his life, for the sake of human sin, and let us not forget it for a moment."[16] This means that faithful, incarnational presence must be accompanied by a willingness to suffer for others. "We cannot have an incarnation," Melba Maggay writes, "without experiencing some form of crucifixion."[17] We must learn to endure this path not because we are masochists but because we are following Jesus.

As we follow Jesus, his way may call us to suffer on behalf of others. Just as Christ was crucified for the world, we are also called to take up the cross for the world. Just as the shame and suffering of Christ lead to the salvation of humanity, our sacrificial shame and suffering can lead others to Christ. The paradox of the Christian experience is that our willingness to suffer is an important ingredient of our witness (Greek, *martyrion*; Acts 1:8). In other words, we do not suffer for the sake of suffering but, rather, for the sake of demonstrating that Jesus's way of giving himself for others is part of his way, which is the truth of life. The ministry of reconciliation is a ministry of solidarity and advocacy for others, even at the cost of our honor and lives. Following the priestly Jesus is to join him in offering ourselves as sacrifices when reconciliation calls for it—which requires a willingness to walk the way of suffering.

Surprisingly, the best examples—among his twelve disciples—of following Jesus in his suffering and death are Peter and another, unnamed disciple (John 18:15). Peter made a heartfelt vow in John 13:37: "Lord, why can't I follow you now? I will lay down my life for you." The realization of Peter's impulsive promise would have to wait until after he received the empowerment of the Holy Spirit (having denied Jesus [John 18:17–18, 25–27]). Nevertheless, the fact that Peter was willing to follow Jesus after his arrest indicates much

---

16. Gunton, "One Mediator," 155.
17. Melba Padilla Maggay, PhD, *Transforming Society: Reflections on the Kingdom and Politics* (Quezon City, Philippines: Institute for Studies in Asian Church and Culture, 2004), 111.

courage. Peter followed the road to the cross. In the words of John Paul Heil, "with regard to discipleship, although Peter denies being a disciple of Jesus, he has entered the courtyard-sheepfold as one of the sheep for whom Jesus lays down his own life as the good shepherd/high priest, so that Peter can become a shepherd who lays down his life for others."[18]

Following Jesus—the priest who suffers on behalf of others—is not merely a personal calling. It is also the calling of the church as a body. So how does the church as a community follow the sacrificial nature of priestly reconciliation? There are many possible responses to this question, but I would like to look at the church's attitude toward expense and comfort. Jan Vankrunkelsven's critique encapsulates the concern I want to raise: "Gifts to the mission are swallowed up in extravagant piles of bricks and concrete of restricted usefulness."[19] This is not an abstract complaint.

Last time I returned to the local church I grew up in, the congregation's project was to install air conditioning at the church. This is a congregation that has been stagnant for fifteen years, with fewer than thirty regular worship attenders. Following Jesus as a church means learning to sacrificially give up the comforts of soft-padded pews and the prestige of owning high-tech equipment in order to prioritize the needs of others. We should all wonder, especially those of us who are pastors and church leaders, if our good intention of providing a comfortable and relaxing worship experience is actually producing a group of Christians who are self-centered, apathetic, and pleasure-oriented.

One ahead of Us

The priestly role of Jesus in our reconciliation with God does not end with the cross. Although the book of Hebrews asserts that his sacrifice is once and for all and all sufficient (10:1–14), it also emphasizes that his reconciling work is still ongoing. The good news is that Jesus is our mediator even today as the ascended Lord. The New Testament refers to the priestly Jesus at the presence of the Father as humanity's intercessor (Rom. 8:34; Heb. 7:23–25) and advocate (1 John 2:1). The conclusions by Richard

---

18. John Paul Heil, "Jesus as the Unique High Priest in the Gospel of John," *The Catholic Biblical Quarterly* 57 (1995), 745.

19. Jan Vankrunkelsven, "Realities and Duties of the Incarnate Church," *African Ecclesiastical Review* 12 (1970), 156.

D. Nelson on the role of high priest in the *Yom Kippur* explain the salvific importance of the ascension. Using Old Testament templates of sacrifice from Leviticus 16:15–16 and Exodus 24:3–8, Nelson argues that Christ's sacrificial act can be divided into three stages: 1) the death of the victim; 2) the passage of the priest into the realm of the holy; and 3) the use of blood to effect forgiveness and renew covenantal relationships. In short, the death of the sacrifice is not the end of the atoning process. The most important part of the *at-one-ment* is the actual, physical presence of the high priest in the Holy of Holies sprinkling the blood of the sacrificial animal.[20] This act of atonement is precisely what Jesus the High Priest does for us even today.

Jesus, our High Priest, is now at the true Holy of Holies, sprinkling his sacrificial blood for the forgiveness of our sins. He did not enter the presence of the Father empty-handed—because "it is necessary for this priest . . . to have something to offer" (Heb. 8:3, NRSV). He brought his own blood, shed on the cross, as the sacrificial gift (9:12, 14; 10:19; 13:12). Jesus is the priest *and* the sacrifice. To put it another way, our High Priest is with the Father, continuously offering himself as the sacrifice so that our sins are continuously forgiven. The cross and the ascension are logically connected because the king who established peace in the kingdom has the complementary duty to continuously maintain it.[21]

So how does Jesus maintain the peace between God and humanity? Hebrews 7:23–25 interprets the saving work of the ascended Christ as the ministry of intercession. In the same way that Jesus represented humanity to the Father at the cross, Jesus is representing humanity before the Father's throne of grace. Like the high priest who entered the Holy of Holies with a breastplate covered with the names of the twelve tribes of Israel, Jesus brings humanity with him in his heart before the Father. The content of Jesus's intercession is also the same prayer he prayed when he was on the cross at Golgotha: "Father, forgive them, for they do not know what they are doing" (Luke 23:34). Jesus intercedes for us and on our behalf because he knows that we are humans who are prone to sin. Paul's summary is remarkable: "Who is to condemn? Christ Jesus is the one who died—more than that, who was raised—who is at the right hand of God, who indeed is

---

20. Richard D. Nelson, "'He Offered Himself': Sacrifice in Hebrews," *Interpretations* 57 (2003), 251–65.

21. Khobnya, "Reconciliation Must Prevail," 131.

interceding for us" (Rom. 8:34, ESV). Jesus knows us better than we know ourselves. He knows our tendencies and inclinations, which is why he ascended into heaven to continue his saving work by being our advocate. A lengthy quotation from Noel Due beautifully expresses the gospel of Jesus the ascended priest:

> He knows what it is like for us when we are passing through the darkest of our dark nights. He knows what it is like when we are faced with the very real prospect of death. He has not expunged that from his memory. The man Jesus is able to sympathise with us in heaven because he has come through and lived through every pain and torment that you could imagine the human heart would come through; testing and trials and suffering we could barely imagine impinged on him almost every moment of the day. He knows what it is like to come through and so he does not condemn us. When sometimes we are troubled or perplexed or the spectre of death looms large and we are a little bit reluctant, or when we have to learn to trust God in the middle of the darkness, he knows what it is like and he does not send us out of the classroom if we blot our copybook. He is not ashamed to call us his brothers and sisters. He knows what it is like to be betrayed by one of his closest associates and I daresay his closest friends. He knows what it is like to be on the receiving end of deceit and injustice and undeserved hostility and undeserved persecution. He knows what it is like to be condemned to death not for his own sins, but for the sins of others.[22]

Vital to the priestly mediation of the ascended Jesus is his life as the incarnate Son. The book of Hebrews places strong emphasis on the fact that Jesus is able to empathize with our weaknesses precisely because he was "one who has been tempted in every way, just as we are" (4:15). Jesus intercedes for us and is our advocate before the Father because he knows the difficulties and challenges of human life. "Because he himself suffered when he was tempted," Hebrews 2:18 says, "he is able to help those who are being tempted."

With these considerations, the ministry of reconciliation entrusted to Jesus's followers becomes clear as the ministry of patient and continuous intercession and advocacy. At their core, our daily experiences as humans on earth are no different from others, regardless of geographical, racial,

---

22. Noel Due, "Christ Ascended for Us—'Jesus Our Ascended High Priest,'" *Evangel* 25 (Summer 2007), 57.

gender, economic, or age differences. Following Jesus, who chooses not to condemn—because he knows our struggles and weaknesses—means that we ought to empathize with others in their brokenness and intercede for them for their forgiveness. Instead of a holier-than-thou attitude, we must have an abiding compassion to "snatch them in pity from sin and the grave," to "weep o'er the erring one," and to "lift up the fallen."[23] The ministry of reconciliation is the ministry of faithful, incarnational presence and compassionate advocacy.

Moreover, because the work of the priestly Jesus is to go to the presence of the Father ahead of us in order to establish the possibility of our own entrance into the Holy of Holies, we too serve as guides to the lost. We must not forget that one of the ultimate consequences of the priestly work of Jesus is so that humanity may "approach God's throne of grace with confidence, so that we may receive mercy and find grace to help us in our time of need" (Heb. 4:16). The ministry of reconciliation entrusted to us is to usher people to the place where Jesus is: the embracing presence of God. People will remain aloof to the gospel as long as the church continues to be a place where people feel condemned because of their sins. The ministry of reconciliation invites the weak, the lowly, the struggling—just as we all are—by making the church and our homes centers of grace and kindness. Our sanctuaries should be filled with so much love and advocacy that sinners will not feel dreadfully intimidated to enter.

There is also something unique about imitating Jesus's ministry of reconciliation as the ascended priest. Whereas following Jesus's incarnational ministry requires us to be with the people, following Jesus's intercessional ministry mostly happens when we are not with others—literally ministry-in-absence. Our priestly ministry does not end the moment we enter our cars to drive home. Jesus was a priest in the house of Zacchaeus the sinner, in the streets filled with the sick, in the fields with the hungry, and in the presence of the Father. Like Jesus, we are priests not only on the street or in the sanctuary but also in front of our computers and on our phones as we read and write Facebook posts. We are priests when we stand and sit with people and when we are on our knees alone. We are priests both in the presence of the needy, publicly, and in the presence of the Father, privately. This reality

23. Frances J. (Fanny) Crosby, "Rescue the Perishing." Printed in *Sing to the Lord* (Kansas City: Lillenas, 1993) as Hymn #713.

requires us to have the gift of reflective recollection. Priestly intercession requires remembering others, along with their needs and circumstances. This is what it means to follow and imitate Jesus, our own Priest.

Conclusions

The threads that run through Jesus's way of priestly reconciliation are solidarity, representation, and faithful intercession. In his faithful, incarnate presence, he is both one of us and one with us so that he might lift us up to God. He initiates the process of reconciliation. We are reconciled to God because God first chooses to be "God with us." In his crucifixion, he suffered on our behalf and for our sakes so that, through his blood, we might receive peace. Again, God took the initiative in laying down his life as a ransom for the forgiveness of our sins because, without forgiveness, there will be no restoration of relationship. In his ascension, Jesus intercedes for us and paves the way so that we too might boldly approach the throne of grace. Jesus is not content to empty himself in the incarnation and to humble himself even to death; he ultimately ascends to the Father in order to become our advocate. He does all of this so that we might be reconciled to God.

Following and imitating Jesus, therefore, and participating in the ministry of reconciliation entail our faithful solidarity and advocacy—even at the cost of shame and suffering—with those we hope are reconciled to God. We do this both when we are with others and also when we are alone in our prayer rooms. We must be healed of our cold, individualistic isolation from others in our own communities. We must be transformed from our self-centeredness and learn to think of ourselves as being for others. We must allow the Spirit of love to kindle compassion in our apathetic hearts. We must search our innermost thoughts and attitudes with ruthless honesty regarding how we treat others, how we use our limited resources, and how we work in the kingdom of God.

The way of reconciliation is extremely relational, which is why, as Ferdinand Nwaigbo asserts, the community is the "locus of reconciliation."[24] Only in the context of communal embrace can people be reconciled to God and others. Only when our churches possess an active, community-constituting mindset can we accomplish—as the body of Christ—our

---

24. Nwaigbo, "Christ Jesus," 374.

mandate as ministers of reconciliation. Only when Christlike generosity, kindness, and loving inclusiveness characterize our Christian communities can we expect others to believe in the biblical message of reconciliation. Only when we embody the reconciled life in our different relationships—familial, filial, and ecclesial—do we have the integrity to become ministers of reconciliation.

8 ✝ FOLLOWING JESUS'S WAY OF HOLINESS

Gift Mtukwa

WHEN we talk about Jesus as a priest, part of what we are saying is that he connects us to the holy. Priests have long been understood to act as those who can mediate the holy to us, connecting us to a beautiful and divine mystery that changes us as we encounter it. But Jesus is a priest in a unique way because an encounter with Jesus is an encounter with holiness itself. Jesus does not mediate the holy to us, as if holiness were some far-away reality, coming to us through a pipe. Rather, Jesus offers us his entire life, which is holiness with us in the flesh. The possibilities and promise of encountering holiness through such a different kind of priest deserve our attention.

Holiness encountered in the priesthood of Jesus is a major concern of the book of Hebrews. In fact, the entire argument of the book depends on the portrait of Jesus as high priest (2:17–18).[1] Jesus as high priest not only connects us to the holy but also enables us to be holy. Written to what was essentially a house church, Hebrews issues a call to an encounter with the great High Priest and, in that encounter, to know the promise of living in the light of holiness.

---

1. Kevin Lee Anderson, *Hebrews: A Commentary in the Wesleyan Tradition* (Kansas City: Beacon Hill Press of Kansas City, 2013), 235. F. F. Bruce, *The Epistle to the Hebrews, Revised Edition, The New International Commentary on the New Testament* (Grand Rapids: Eerdmans, 1990), 115.

Jesus the Suffering, Tempted High Priest

The holiness we encounter in Jesus's life is not a sanctity requiring separation, cleanly removed from the suffering of the world; rather, it is a holiness that actively engages the world. While we may consider priests to be holy because they are untouched by the temptations of the world around them, Jesus provides a new vision of the way priests convey holiness. The vision of holiness mediated to us by Jesus is a kind that does not shy away from suffering and temptation, as if he floated, unscathed, above human experience. Rather, the holiness Jesus opens to us is holiness that steps into suffering and temptation, overcoming it without avoiding it.

Early in the letter, the author of Hebrews introduces the theme of Jesus as high priest with the intention of demonstrating how this high priest opens holiness to us in a profound way. Certainly, a high priest is one who is "exalted above the heavens" (7:26), yet this high priest is simultaneously one who is able to be sympathetic to us because he refuses to escape the pain of suffering and temptation, choosing instead to enter completely into it.

As a priest, Jesus was made like his brothers and sisters "in order that he might become a merciful and faithful high priest" (2:17). Unlike the sort of priests in ancient and modern contexts who suppose that holiness requires them to separate themselves from the people in order to minister to them, Jesus offers a radically different priesthood. Jesus becomes like his brothers and sisters so that he might minister to them.[2]

What makes Christ's high priesthood great is that he has been "exalted above the heavens" (7:26).[3] Hebrews 4:15 (NRSV) states, "For we do not have a high priest who is unable to sympathize with our weaknesses," making use of a double negative as a way of emphasizing the point that Christ is indeed able to sympathize with humanity because his high priesthood is not one of separation but, rather, is one of engagement.[4] The highness that we tend to

---

2. Craig R. Koester, *Hebrews: A New Translation with Introduction and Commentary*, vol. 36, *Anchor Yale Bible Commentaries* (Doubleday, 2001), 241. Pere A. Vanhoye, "Situation et Signification de Hébreux v. 1–10," *New Testament Studies* 23.04 (1977): 368. According to Patrick Gray, Jesus is the ideal brother to whom Plutarch refers. Gray, "Brotherly Love," 335–51.

3. Bruce, *Epistle to the Hebrews*, 115.

4. Fred B. Craddock, "The Letter to the Hebrews," *The New Interpreter's Bible: New Testament Survey* (Nashville: Abingdon, 2006).

associate with holiness is not the only component of his priesthood. Perhaps the most striking component is the remarkable, beautiful, and mysterious reality that God's holiness can be seen in the way Jesus engages the places, issues, and persons generally considered to be most unholy.

The transcendence of Christ does not make him less human. Rather, he makes use of his transcendence in an ultimately priestly way, becoming the living link between holiness itself and a creation in need of an encounter with a holy God. The author of Hebrews makes it clear that the "merciful and faithful high priest" was like his brothers and sisters in every way and "is able to help those who are being tempted" since "he himself suffered when he was tempted" (2:17–18). By stepping into the human situation and mediating holiness by being present in the persistent, unholy evil that threatens to undo humans, "Jesus exemplifies the best of priestly tradition."[5]

The English word "sympathize" may be so common that we forget its significance; the Greek word used in Hebrews (*sympatheō*) entails being affected by another's troubles.[6] Jesus not only understands but also is able to empathize and have compassion. He is one who suffered, he can identify with the problems of others, and he is able "to bring support and assistance to them."[7] The reason Christ can sympathize is that he was "tempted in every way, *just as we are*—yet he did not sin" (4:15, emphasis added).

The fact that Christ endured temptation and did not sin is critical for our Christian understanding of what it means to be human, a realm of study often referred to as *theological anthropology*. The primary takeaway here is that Jesus defines what it means to be fully alive as a human. He endures temptation, yes, but he also demonstrates that falling to temptation is not what makes a person human. The *fullness* of humanity is found in the holiness that Jesus mediates to us—a life lived not floating above temptation but remaining faithful to God *in the midst* of it. Since Christ endured temptation and did not sin, his priestly ministry opens a new way for us to think of being human, which is not defined according to being overcome by temptation. While we all experience the temptation to sin, the ministry

---

5. Koester, *Hebrews*, 241.

6. The verb *patheō* describes the act of suffering or feeling, while its prefix *sym/syn* means "with" or "alongside."

7. Anderson, *Hebrews*, 159.

of a high priest who became like us and endured temptation but did not sin mediates to us the powerful possibility of living without being defined as a human *by* sin; that is, Jesus presents the possibility of a life of holiness.

"Jesus experienced the full ambiguity and uncertainty, the weakness and the vulnerability, the temptations and the sufferings of life without compromising his humanity," D. Stephen Long reminds us, "without straying from his calling to be a human being."[8] Our High Priest entered into the same kind of temptation that we regularly encounter, but he mediates holiness in doing so. He does not turn away from faithfulness when temptation beckons. Jesus is a priest *par excellence* because he has partaken of the very intricacies of human existence—including enduring temptation.[9]

The humanity of Christ does not contradict his sinlessness because sinfulness is not intrinsic to what it means to be fully human.[10] The popular phrase "to err is human" is actually refuted by the fully human Jesus, who endures pain and temptation but does not sin. The author of Hebrews also disagrees with that age-old cliché, offering instead a vision of Jesus as a priest who has known our struggle intimately and has emerged victoriously. The readers of Hebrews are likewise encouraged, even when facing similar temptations to turn away from God and neglect their faith.

The enduring promise of Jesus's priestly work is that he "became what we are in order to make us what he is himself."[11] The two adjectives (merciful and faithful) help him to relate to his brothers and sisters (merciful) and to God (faithful).[12] Jesus can offer mercy to fellow humans because he has been where they are and can understand them. Although humanity in Adam became faithless, in Christ it becomes faithful.

In Jesus's priestly ministry, holiness is thrown open to us, and we are invited to enter in. This invitation comes as an obvious contrast to aspects of the Levitical priesthood, in which protecting the holy dwelling place

---

8. D. Stephen Long, *Hebrews* (Louisville: Westminster John Knox Press, 2011), 64.

9. Anderson, *Hebrews*, 159.

10. Donald A. Hagner, *Encountering the Book of Hebrews: An Exposition* (Grand Rapids: Baker Academic, 2002), 78.

11. Michael Welker and Cynthia A. Jarvis, ed., *Loving God with Our Minds: The Pastor as Theologian* (Grand Rapids: Eerdmans, 2004), 326.

12. Ben Witherington III, *Letters and Homilies for Jewish Christians: A Socio-Rhetorical Commentary on Hebrews, James and Jude* (Downers Grove, IL: IVP Academic, 2007). Hagner, *Encountering the Book of Hebrews*, 61.

of God meant sealing it off from the unholy. The stunning invitation of Hebrews 4:16 beckons readers to "approach God's throne of grace with confidence, so that we may receive mercy and find grace to help us in our time of need." Jesus alone was able to do the kind of priestly work that does not set an encounter with the holy behind a barricade but, rather, flings open the door and invites a live encounter with living holiness. It is Jesus's unique priestly role that makes holiness about mercy and grace. "Our great high priest," Kevin Anderson observes, "who is completely 'set apart from sinners' and 'exalted above the heavens,' possesses the unlimited resources of holiness to save his people completely from sin (7:25–26)."[13] The astonishing difference between Jesus and other priests, however, is that his being set apart and exalted was not a step out of the fleshly, worldly mess of pain and temptation. Instead he was set apart to step into the world, bringing all the resources of holiness to bear on a world that could not heal itself. Since people can approach the throne of grace through Jesus's priestly ministry, they do so confidently, having acquired the holiness that was formerly the preserve of the Levitical priest. Christ's sacrifice is what has made the difference for those who would approach the very abode of God, the place where holiness lives.

Christ the Perfect Priest and His Sacrifice

We should also say a few words about the way Jesus deals with sacrifice as a priest who mediates holiness. You may recall that Israel's priestly vocation called for a good deal of sacrificing, usually of animals that were without blemish. This long-standing practice was not only a mark of their holiness as God's chosen people, but worked to preserve their holiness when their actions did not measure up to their chosenness (Exod. 12:5; Lev. 1:3).

Hebrews contrasts the priesthood of ordinary priests and that of Jesus, while also demonstrating how Jesus fulfills priestly sacrifice in a way the priestly system could not. The ordinary priests "offer gifts and sacrifices for sins" (5:1), whereas Christ offers "prayers and petitions" (v. 7) because Christ has no sins of his own for which he needs to provide sacrifices. When the author of Hebrews goes on to refer to Jesus as the one who "offered himself unblemished to God," we can be sure that a fulfillment is taking place.

---

13. Anderson, *Hebrews*, 159.

Now Jesus is both the priest *and* the sacrifice, whose self-sacrificial ministry results in cleansing from "acts that lead to death, so that we may serve the living God" (9:14). In short, by offering himself as a sacrifice, he opens to us the possibility for the fullness of life that comes with joyful service to God—the life of holiness. For the author of Hebrews, this is nothing short of the goal of salvation. Salvation in Hebrews certainly includes the forgiveness of sins (10:18), but it is not complete without sanctification—that is, being made holy through Christ's priestly sacrifice (10:10).

As a priest, Jesus has "become the guarantee of a better covenant" (7:22, NRSV). In the Old Testament, the covenant was about a relationship between God and his people; such a covenant required the people to be holy. Now that there is a better covenant, or new covenant, there is a new possibility for the people to be God's holy people. Echoing the cries of the prophet Jeremiah, the author of Hebrews speaks of a people who live the abundant life of holiness and of the joys of knowing God deeply "from the least of them to the greatest" (8:11).

What the prophets could only anticipate is now a reality through what Christ has done: the perfect priest has become the unblemished sacrifice, and his sacrifice extends to us the possibility of the delight of holiness. "Because of the perfectness of his obedience," Robert H. Culpepper states, "because Christ is the lamb without spot or blemish, his sacrifice is received by God. But because our lives are polluted by sin we dare not offer ourselves."[14] Christ has done something that other priests could not do; instead of entering the Holy of Holies, he has entered the heavenly tabernacle itself.[15] He has entered with his own blood, not the blood of bulls and goats (9:12, 24), and the result has a way for those who were living at a distance from God's life-giving presence to draw near in confidence and experience the joy of living. In this way, those who worship God are perfected and made fit to approach God (9:9, 14; 10:2, 22).[16]

---

14. Robert H. Culpepper, *Interpreting the Atonement* (Raleigh, NC: Stevens Books, 1966), 153.

15. Paul Ellingworth, *The Epistle to the Hebrews: A Commentary on the Greek Text*, *The New International Greek Testament Commentary* series (Grand Rapids: Eerdmans, 1993), 452.

16. Anderson, *Hebrews*, 267. Michael Keenan Jones, *Jesus Our Priest: A Christian Approach to the Priesthood of Christ* (Oxford: Oxford University Press, 2010), 54.

The atonement is not a matter of moral privilege for a few but concerns a reality of human existence: we are all dragged down by sin. Sin is anything that pulls us away from God and the life God is giving. The good news we receive in Jesus's priesthood is that the Son of God—peerless among humans in his holiness—gives himself so that we sinners may be made holy and approach God's "throne of grace" (4:16).[17] Whereas previous attempts to address the problem of sin were merely temporary, Christ's sacrifice is final and deals with sin conclusively. Until Jesus, humans provided the sacrifice, but in his self-sacrificial priesthood, the final sacrifice is provided by God.[18] This is the priestly ministry that is done "on our behalf," even though it comes at God's great expense (9:24, NRSV).

Encountering Holiness through Jesus's Priesthood

Holiness is not a moralistic abstraction but a real, live possibility. This is why the writer of Hebrews does not discuss the priesthood of Christ abstractly but speaks of Christ's priesthood in direct relation to the day-to-day realities of those who are under the ministry of the great High Priest. In other words, everything that followers of Jesus have been called to become has been offered to us in his own self-sacrificial priesthood. What the church is called to become is made possible by having Christ as a high priest. Since the followers of Jesus have been called to be holy, holiness is not something God demands without offering a way forward. Since it is the fullness of life, holiness is not drudgery but the joyful and robust result of an encounter with the life-giving God. But this holiness is a continual and ongoing gift that has been given through a priest who gave himself.[19] Our hope of holiness came about be-

---

17. See Anderson, *Hebrews*, 233.

18. H. Ray Dunning, *Grace, Faith, & Holiness: A Wesleyan Systematic Theology* (Kansas City: Beacon Hill Press of Kansas City, 1988), 381–82.

19. In Hebrews 10:10, the author uses a perfect passive participle of the verb *hagiazō*, which indicates that the people of God have already been sanctified (*hēgiasmenoi*) by the blood of Christ. The perfect tense *hēgiasmenoi* ("having been sanctified") reveals that this past sanctification has implications for the present. The passive voice is significant because it means the people do not sanctify themselves; it is clear we are dealing with a divine passive, an action done by God. This, however, does not mean the people are unwilling participants; they are recipients of God's action on their behalf.

cause a perfect priest offered his own body as a perfect sacrifice, fulfilling his "vocation as the unblemished sacrifice for sin."[20]

Being made holy through Jesus's priestly ministry does not make us less human but is "the fulfillment or *consummation* of men and women in a permanent, direct and personal relationship with God."[21] The perfection of the people has its basis in the "perfecting of Christ," who is the priestly connection to God.[22] According to Hebrews 2:11, Jesus is the sanctified sanctifier, who shares the same Father with the brothers and sisters he sanctifies.

If, in the Levitical system, the blood of goats and bulls sanctified the defiled (Heb. 9:13), the question for the author of Hebrews is "How much more, then, will the blood of Christ . . . cleanse our consciences from acts that lead to death?" (v. 14). This question requires no answer; its obvious implication is that the blood of Christ is able to do much more than that of bulls and goats. The blood of Christ is able to bring about the inner transformation of the worshiper. In other words, it provides for the cleansing of the conscience and the joyful service of God.

The gift of holiness that Jesus offers in his own priestly sacrifice is an ongoing promise, a gift that continues to be given. According to Hebrews, believers have not only *been* sanctified, but they are also "*being* sanctified" (10:14, ESV, emphasis added).[23] The forms of *hagiazō* (meaning "I make holy") that the author uses in Hebrews 10 indicate "that Christians have been sanctified and are being sanctified" through Christ's priestly ministry.[24] While this is interesting on linguistic terms alone, it also points to a profound aspect of what it means to consider Jesus as priest: he shares holiness with us in a constant and ongoing act of giving, making us "holy partners in a heavenly calling" (3:1, NRSV). Jesus's desire is that his brothers and sisters "may share in his holiness" (12:10). Jesus's priestly act was to

---

20. Gordon J. Thomas, "The Perfection of Christ and the Perfecting of Believers in Hebrews" in *Holiness and Ecclesiology in the New Testament*, ed. Kent E. Brower and Andy Johnson (Grand Rapids: Eerdmans, 2007), 297.

21. David Peterson, *Possessed by God: A New Testament Theology of Sanctification and Holiness* (Downers Grove, IL: InterVarsity Press, 2000), 33–36.

22. Ibid.

23. Robert Jewett, *Letter to Pilgrims: A Commentary on the Epistle to the Hebrews* (Cleveland: Pilgrim Press, 1981), 304. The present participle of *hagiazō*, which is *hagiazomenous*, speaks of the ongoing nature of the sanctification.

24. Thomas, "The Perfection of Christ," 304.

share in what we were, that we might share in what he is. The call to holiness, then, is not merely a call to try as hard as we can on our own to clean up our behavior, but it is the call to share in the very character of God.[25] Holiness belongs to God alone, but in Jesus's priestly act of making himself the perfect sacrifice, he allows the people to partake.[26]

Of course, holiness is far more than a kind of ritualized right standing before God. While sanctification includes being in right relationship with God, it also includes a moral dimension: it not only does something to our relationship with God, but it does something to the way we relate to others as well. For example, in Hebrews 12:14, the people of faith are called to pursue peace and holiness together. Gordon Thomas is right when he observes, "If the essence of holiness is a right relationship with a holy God, then the vital, tangible expression of holiness is right relationships with other people."[27] The priestly ministry of Jesus opens an encounter with holiness that changes us—but not only as individuals. His ministry also opens to us the beautiful possibility of being at peace with one another, a sure testimony to holiness. When the people of God are truly holy and live peacefully in full view of the world, then they are to be "the true high priestly people of God," in the words of Justin Martyr.[28]

The present and ongoing moral effect of Jesus's priestly ministry also begins to make us holy as he is holy. Since his holiness cannot be held apart from his self-sacrifice, to share in his holiness is to share in his pattern of sacrifice. Following our great High Priest, the people of God are to take upon themselves the posture of sacrifice. He offered himself; so should his followers. Gerald O'Collins and Michael Keenan Jones describe the call to believers in Hebrews: "They are called to a priestly existence that involves ongoing sacrifice not only through their prayers of praise and confession of faith but through 'doing good' and generously sharing with others."[29] Such sacrificial living takes concrete shape as they love one another, welcome

---

25. Timothy Friberg, Barbara Friberg, and Neva F. Miller, *Analytical Lexicon of the Greek New Testament* (Victoria, BC: Trafford Publishing, 2005).

26. William L. Lane, *Hebrews 9–13*, vol. 47b, *Word Biblical Commentary* (Grand Rapids: Zondervan, 1991), 425.

27. Thomas, "The Perfection of Christ," 309.

28. *Dialogue with Trypho*, 116.1.3.

29. Gerald O'Collins, SJ, and Michael Keenan Jones, *Jesus Our Priest: A Christian Approach to the Priesthood of Christ* (Oxford: Oxford University Press, 2012), 56.

strangers, care for prisoners, live faithfully in marriage, and avoid materialism (13:1–5). The "living sacrifice" of Romans 12:1 is equivalent to the "acceptable worship" of Hebrews 12:28 (NRSV).[30]

Holiness in Hebrews is a gift that is provided by God since it is God's essential attribute.[31] God's Son, Jesus Christ, provides holiness graciously through his death, and we are its undeserving recipients. The people of God are to pursue it as the ultimate goal, yet realizing that it has been given already. All humanity can do is accept it. God is the one who makes men and women holy (10:10, 14). The requirement to be holy is not an afterthought, but, rather, a result of God's desire for humans. Holiness is both a gift and a task; yes, it has been given, but, according to Hebrews, Christians must pursue it. The holy people of God are to take the posture of sacrifice, which their High Priest took upon himself. To follow Jesus, according to Hebrews, is to be willing to suffer and accept the discipline of God.

Implications for the Church

Holiness is not optional for Christians. For those who follow Jesus as priest, holiness is the mode of our relationship with God and with one another. Holiness is not something that one denomination chooses to make their distinctive doctrine; rather, it is what God desires for every Christian regardless of their theological tradition. Jesus our priest teaches us that sin is not what defines human beings and that a life without sin is indeed possible. In this day and age in which sin has been accepted as a normal part of life, Hebrews presents the possibility of a life where sin is not part of the equation. For those who will be content with a past sanctification, Hebrews reminds us of an ongoing and dynamic life of holiness. The balance between what God does and what we do must be maintained. God provides sanctification and holiness that must be pursued, realizing it has been given already.

The relationship between peace and holiness is crucial for the twenty-first-century church. We cannot claim to have a good relationship with God while failing to foster relationships with our brothers and sisters. The holy people of God ought to desire wholeness for all people and the created order. Our relationships can be a barometer for measuring our holiness. However,

---

30. Ibid.
31. Lane, *Hebrews 9–13*, 450.

we must remember that holiness in the way of the great High Priest must be according to his distinctive way. While holiness results in peaceful relationships, it cannot be confused with simply "getting along" with ways of life that are actively opposed to Jesus's distinct way. For example, those who live in cultures with a communal worldview (most sub-Saharan tribes) should not sacrifice a relationship with God in order to be acceptable to the community.

In sub-Saharan Africa, the traditional religions often hold sway over Christians. There are cases of some within the church who frequent traditional shrines to seek help from religious practitioners. Hebrews tells us our own High Priest, Christ Jesus, is sufficient, and he provides not only a better hope but also a better sacrifice. Holiness, in this context, means we reject any form of apostasy and hold on to Jesus, "who is the author and perfecter of faith" (12:2, NASB).

Conclusion

Hebrews reveals that Jesus is a perfect priest and a perfect sacrifice. He had no sin yet is able to sympathize with us, and his sacrifice is effective, able to deal conclusively with sin and provide purification. Christ's priestly ministry provides holiness, enabling people to come before the throne of grace, where they can see God. Holiness in Hebrews is not just about purity in worship; it also has ethical significance. It is about how we take the sacrificial posture upon ourselves in the manner in which our priest did. Holiness is about how we love one another, live with the stranger, care for the prisoners, and live faithfully in marriage. May the church of the twenty-first century experience the reality David Peterson expresses so well: "When the sanctifying work of Jesus is proclaimed and believed, God changes our hearts and binds us to himself as children of the New Covenant."[32]

Suggestions for Further Reading

Anderson, Kevin Lee. *Hebrews: A Commentary in the Wesleyan Tradition*. Kansas City: Beacon Hill Press of Kansas City, 2013.

Greathouse, William M. *Wholeness in Christ: Toward a Biblical Theology of Holiness*. Kansas City: Beacon Hill Press of Kansas City, 1998.

Isaacs, Marie E. "Priesthood and the Epistle to the Hebrews." *Heythrop Journal* 38.1 (1997): 51–62.

---

32. Peterson, *Possessed by God*, 40.

Jewett, Robert. *Letter to Pilgrims: A Commentary on the Epistle to the Hebrews.* New York: Pilgrim Press, 1981.

Koester, Craig R. *Hebrews: A New Translation with Introduction and Commentary.* Vol. 36. *Anchor Yale Bible Commentaries.* Doubleday, 2001.

Leclerc, Diane. *Discovering Christian Holiness: The Heart of Wesleyan-Holiness Theology.* Kansas City: Beacon Hill Press of Kansas City, 2013.

Long, D. Stephen. *Hebrews.* Louisville: Westminster John Knox Press, 2011.

Peterson, David. *Possessed by God: A New Testament Theology of Sanctification and Holiness.* Downers Grove, IL: InterVarsity Press, 2000.

Westcott, Brooke Foss. *The Epistle to the Hebrews: The Greek Texts with Notes and Essays.* Whitefish, MT: Kessinger, 2003.

Witherington, Ben III. *Letters and Homilies for Jewish Christians: A Socio-Rhetorical Commentary on Hebrews, James and Jude.* Downers Grove, IL: IVP Academic, 2007.

9 ✝ FOLLOWING JESUS AS KING

David Young

JESUS CHRIST. These words appear together so many times in the New Testament that it is easy for them to become inseparable in the minds of many readers. One can become so accustomed to seeing them together that it may not even occur to us to ask what they mean. Indeed, I suspect many readers simply regard this as Jesus's full name. That is, "Christ" is Jesus's surname in the same way that Young is my surname.

In fact, "Christ" is more like an honorific title.[1] *Christos* is the Greek equivalent of the Hebrew word *Messiah* (*mashiach*). In the most basic sense, both words refer to someone who has been anointed with oil. In ancient Israel, one could be anointed with oil for a number of reasons, usually signaling that the person had been selected for a specific and important task.[2] Priests were anointed for their tasks in the tabernacle or temple (Exod. 29:7; Lev. 6:20–22; 8:12). Prophets could be anointed to speak the word of God to the people of Israel (Isa. 61:1). Even certain objects could be anointed with oil in order to mark them as holy implements set aside for a specific purpose (Exod. 40:1–11; Num. 7:1–88).

---

1. Matthew V. Novenson, *Christ among the Messiahs: Christ Language in Paul and Messiah Language in Ancient Judaism* (New York: Oxford University Press, 2012), 95.

2. K. M. Heim, "Kings and Kingship" in Bill T. Arnold and H. G. M. Williamson, eds., *Dictionary of the Old Testament: Historical Books*, Student Edition (Downers Grove, IL: IVP Academic, 2005), 620.

However, the term is most commonly associated with those who were anointed to be king. In 1 Samuel 10, Samuel anoints Saul as king over Israel. Only six chapters later, he anoints David as Saul's replacement. In many parts of Israel's story, "the Lord's anointed" becomes a virtual synonym for the king of Israel. This is, of course, why this chapter on Jesus as king begins with the term "Christ." In order to understand what it means to call Jesus a king, it is important to have some understanding of why his earliest followers affixed this title to his name. Why did the writers of the New Testament use the phrase "Jesus Messiah" so frequently that it has become easy for later readers, like ourselves, to miss the irony of such a claim? What did the first Christians intend to communicate about Jesus when they referred to him as the anointed king of Israel?

Kingly Ideas in Israel

Christians often talk about Jesus as *the* Messiah, which makes sense within Christian theology, where the uniqueness of Jesus and the singularity of what he accomplished are emphasized. However, it may easily give a wrong impression about messianic expectations within Judaism prior to the time of Jesus. For example, one might easily reason that, if Jesus is *the* Messiah, then Israel had been awaiting a single Messiah throughout its history and that everyone agreed on what that Messiah would look like. Unfortunately, such a notion ignores the way the concept of *messiah* is discussed in the Hebrew scriptures.

Since the word "messiah" simply refers to someone who is anointed for a specific task, there could be any number of messiahs appointed by God to carry out God's purposes. Even when the term was more closely associated with kingly duties, there was not one set of defined parameters for what that kingly role should be. One of the more fascinating uses of the term "messiah" in the Hebrew scriptures occurs in Isaiah 45:1. There, Cyrus, the king of Persia, is referred to as the Lord's anointed (*mashiach*) because he is the one whom God is using to accomplish God's purposes in the world—in this case, returning Israel from exile. The fact that the king of a foreign nation who did not worship Israel's God could be referred to as Yahweh's anointed speaks to just how broadly this category could be stretched. Similarly, the Jewish community that produced the Dead Sea Scrolls in the centuries prior to the time of Jesus appears to have anticipated two messiahs, one kingly in nature and one priestly.[3]

Despite this diversity of opinion about the nature of messiah and king, there are some aspects of kingship that are central for Israel. The first of these is that Israel's true king is, first and foremost, God (see Exod. 15:18; Deut. 10:14–18; Pss. 10:16–18; 29:10–11; 96:10; 145:1–17; Dan. 4:3–37). This tenet can be seen in Isaiah 6, the prophet's well-known vision of Yahweh seated on his throne with the train of God's robe filling the temple. Magnificent creatures cry out, "Holy, holy, holy is the LORD of hosts; the whole earth is full of his glory" (v. 3, NRSV). And Isaiah responds, "Woe is me! I am lost, for I am a man of unclean lips, and I live among a people of unclean lips; *yet my eyes have seen the King, the LORD of hosts!*" (v. 5, NRSV, emphasis added).

Indeed, when the elders of Israel first request a king, the request is interpreted as a rejection of Yahweh's own kingly status over Israel. God declares to the prophet Samuel, "they have not rejected you, but they have rejected me from being king over them" (1 Sam. 8:7, NRSV). This passage is one of many instances in which Israel's scriptures record a critical stance concerning the monarchy. Samuel warns that a king will only tax the people heavily for his own prosperity and take their sons and daughters as his own servants—a critique later echoed in the words of Jeremiah and Ezekiel (see 1 Sam. 8:11–18; Jer. 23:1–4; Ezek. 34:1–6).

In spite of these misgivings about a king, much of Israel's scriptures are filled with the notion that the king served as God's right-hand man, so to speak. This idea is especially apparent in Psalm 110, which begins, "The LORD [God] says to my lord [the king]: 'Sit at my right hand until I make your enemies a footstool for your feet'" (v. 1). The idea in this psalm and others like it seems to be that God works on behalf of his anointed king so that the king can carry out God's reign on earth. The king is a kind of vice-regent, or steward, of God's earthly kingdom. The opening words of Psalm 72 ask God to give the king God's very own justice and righteousness. That request indicates that it was the king's job to be the mediator of God's justice in the world.

---

3. John J. Collins, "Messianism in the Maccabean Period" in Jacob Neusner, William Scott Green, and Ernest S. Frerichs, eds., *Judaisms and Their Messiahs at the Turn of the Christian Era* (New York: Cambridge University Press, 1987), 101–3.

The relationship between Yahweh and the king of Israel was at times understood as being so intimate that the king was described as God's son. In Psalm 2:7, the psalmist writes that God declares to the king, "You are my son; today I have become your father." Likewise, in 2 Samuel 7, when David asks to build a house—that is, a temple for Yahweh—God responds that instead, a house will be built for David: namely, a lineage of kings. Describing David's descendants, God declares, "I will be his father, and he will be my son" (v. 14). Given the strict monotheism of the Hebrew scriptures, it seems unlikely that this meant the king was regarded as divine in the same way as Yahweh. Instead, the language of father and son indicates the bond that Yahweh had made with his chosen one. Indeed, God's promise continues, "My love will never be taken away from him . . . Your house and your kingdom will endure forever before me; your throne will be established forever" (vv. 15–16).

Of course, David's earthly throne was *not* established forever. After Solomon's reign, Scripture records that David's kingdom split in two. A couple centuries later, the northern kingdom, Israel, was destroyed by Assyria. Another century and a half after that, the southern kingdom, Judah, was conquered by Babylon. David's line had come to an end. Nevertheless, Israel's prophets reasoned that this had taken place as punishment for Israel's sin and that, when the time was right, God would send a new king to restore Israel (see, for example, Isa. 11:3–9; Jer. 23:5–7; 33:14–16; Ezek. 34:23–24; Hag. 2:23; Zech. 9:9–10).

After the exile and rebuilding of the temple, there was a period of relative self-governance for the Jewish people under the Maccabees, a priestly family who became royalty after a rebellion.[4] But that autonomy lasted only

---

4. Israel—if it is proper to give that name to the descendants of those who returned from exile in Babylon—would have a king again and would eventually win limited independence centuries later. The background context is that, after the death of Alexander the Great in 323 BCE, his massive empire was divided among his descendants. The territory that had formerly been identified as Israel would change hands between the kingdoms of two of those descendants—dynasties known as the Ptolemies and the Seleucids. In 167 BCE, the Seleucid king, Antiochus IV Epiphanes, desecrated the Jerusalem temple by looting it (1 Macc. 1:20–24; 2 Macc. 5:15–21) and then making it a temple to Zeus, offering impure sacrifices on the altar (1 Macc. 1:54–59; 2 Macc. 6:1–6). This desecration catalyzed a revolt, primarily led by the Jewish priest Mattathias and his sons. One son, Judas Maccabeus, rallied the rebels and, ultimately, defeated the great Seleucid army, bringing about the cleansing and rededication of the temple (which events are memorialized in the

one century (164–63 BCE) before the Romans conquered their land. From that point until the destruction of the temple in 70 CE, any kings of Israel were really only clients of the Romans, put in place to maintain order and raise taxes on behalf of Rome.

The Early Christian Insistence on Jesus's Kingly Nature

Within this mix of ideas about kings and kingdoms, the Gospels tell us that Jesus appears, proclaiming the kingdom of God. Although what has been offered to this point is only a brief survey of the various kingly ideas that existed in ancient Israel, one thing should be relatively obvious to anyone familiar with the story of Jesus: he doesn't really do very kingly things! Jesus does not conquer territory like David or foster prosperity like Solomon. He does not lead a rebellion against the foreign occupying power or save the temple from gentile idolatry. He does not wield political power in any traditional sense of directing armies or controlling the treasury. Jesus is not really in charge of anyone or anything. As far as we can tell, Jesus appears to have been a working-class man who spent most of his time with those who had little to offer in terms of power or wealth in the small towns and villages of Galilee. It might actually be difficult to imagine anyone looking much *less* like a king than Jesus did.

The un-kingly nature of Jesus is nowhere more evidently on display than at his crucifixion. Crucifixion was the surest possible sign that Jesus had failed in his mission as messiah and king. It meant the revolution was over and Rome was victorious once again. The Gospel of Mark tells us that Jesus is mocked with a sign that reads "THE KING OF THE JEWS" (15:26) and that the chief priests and scribes mock him by saying, "Let the Messiah, the King of Israel, come down from the cross now, so that we may see and believe" (v. 32, NRSV). The message is clear: if Jesus is the King he claims to be, God will deliver him from the cross. Mark's radical claim is to flip that conventional wisdom on its head by offering Jesus's suffering and humiliation as a complete and total overhaul of what it means to be king.

---

holiday Hanukkah). Judas's brother Simon ruled after him and was able to establish some measure of independence for Israel. His descendants were known as the Hasmonean dynasty and ruled Israel free of overt foreign interference until the Romans arrived in 63 BCE. For more stories pertaining to the Maccabean Revolt, see the books 1 and 2 Maccabees in the Old Testament Apocrypha.

The crucified Jesus does not in any way appear to be God's right-hand man, administering God's justice and righteousness on earth. And yet the early Christians insisted that is precisely what he was.

In fact, Psalm 110:1, quoted earlier, is the single most frequently quoted verse of the Old Testament in the New Testament. It appears in Matthew, Mark, and Luke as part of Jesus's riddle-like conversation with the religious leaders about the nature of the Messiah, and Jesus alludes to it again at his trial (see Matt. 22:44; 26:64; Mark 12:36; 14:62; Luke 20:42–43; 22:69). Paul also alludes to the verse repeatedly (Rom. 8:34; 1 Cor. 15:25), and it is central to the argument for Jesus's unique status in the epistle to the Hebrews (1:13).[5] Nor is this the only kingly scripture that the New Testament writers apply to Jesus.[6]

Yet alongside these royal passages of Scripture, the New Testament writers also saw Jesus in passages like the Suffering Servant texts of Isaiah 52:13–53:12.[7] Isaiah 53:4–5 (NRSV) states: "Surely he has borne our infirmities and carried our diseases; yet we accounted him stricken, struck down by God, and afflicted. But he was wounded for our transgressions, crushed for our iniquities; upon him was the punishment that made us whole, and by his bruises we are healed." It's easy to see how early Christians saw Jesus as the fulfillment of this text. He had surely suffered, and after the resurrection, they came to see that suffering as redemptive. Such a theology resonates strongly with the words of Isaiah. But here's the catch: it does not appear from the available evidence that anyone else in the first century was reading this passage as a messianic one. It wasn't that these words were commonly accepted as being about the Messiah and all the early Christians had to do was say, "See, Jesus fits the prophecy!" It wasn't that Jesus's followers proclaimed him as Messiah and King because he fit the bill so

---

5. Hebrews also makes use of verse 4 of Psalm 110 in Heb. 5:6, 7:17, and 7:21—the only other New Testament writing to utilize an additional verse from the psalm. See also Acts 2:34–35, Eph. 1:20, and Col. 3:1 for other uses of Ps. 110:1. For more, see David M. Hay, *Glory at the Right Hand: Psalm 110 in Early Christianity* (Atlanta: Society of Biblical Literature, 1973).

6. Hebrews 1 alone provides a stunning list of such passages, including 2 Sam. 7:14 and Pss. 2:7, 45:6–7, 102:25–27, and 104:4.

7. See Matt. 2:23; 26:24, 63, 67; 27:12, 14, 38; Mark 9:12; 14:60–61; Luke 23:33–34; 24:27, 46; John 1:29; Acts 3:13; 10:43; Rom. 4:25; 5:19; 1 Cor. 2:9; 5:7; 15:3; Heb. 9:28; 1 Pet.1:11; 2:23–25; 5:4–5; 1 John 3:5; Rev. 5:6, 12; 13:8; 14:5; 21:19.

perfectly. We have already seen that he clearly did not. Rather, the relationship worked the other way around; early Christians started reading Isaiah 52–53 as messianic *because of their experience of Jesus.* Already convinced Jesus was the Messiah, they began rereading Israel's scriptures in light of what they knew about Jesus. As a result, they saw passages like this one in Isaiah with completely new eyes and began to interpret them in completely new ways. Jesus's redefinition of kingship was so thorough that proclaiming him as King required a complete rereading of the scriptures.

Paul's Messianic Rereading

The rereading of Israel's Scriptures through the lens of Jesus's death and resurrection is fully on display in the writings of Paul. However, when it comes to portraying Jesus as King and Messiah, Paul may also be one of the most enigmatic writers of the New Testament. Paul uses the term "Christ" more than any other New Testament writer, yet, in comparison to the Gospels, his discussions of the kingdom are rare. This reality has left many scholars puzzling over exactly what the term "Christ" meant for Paul.[8] One place Paul does mention the kingdom is 1 Corinthians 15. In verses 24–25 (NRSV), he writes, "Then comes the end, when he hands over the kingdom to God the Father, after he has destroyed every ruler and every authority and power. For he must reign until he has put all his enemies under his feet." In these verses, Paul envisions Jesus handing over the kingdom to God the Father after all his enemies have been defeated, which seems to imply that Jesus's kingdom work has already begun but will not be completed until some time in the future, relative to Paul's writing.

It is fitting that this mention of the kingdom occurs within an extensive discussion of Jesus's resurrection since, for Paul, the resurrection is what sets Jesus apart as God's anointed one. In Romans 1:4 (NRSV), he states that Jesus "was declared to be Son of God with power according to the spirit of holiness by resurrection from the dead, Jesus Christ our Lord." In Paul's theology, Jesus's resurrection signals that he is the Christ—God's anointed. Especially distinctive about Paul's theology is his belief that Jesus's resurrec-

---

8. Novenson, *Christ among the Messiahs*, 2. Andrew Chester, "The Christ of Paul" in Markus Bockmuehl and James Carleton Paget, eds., *Redemption and Resistance: The Messianic Hopes of Jews and Christians in Antiquity* (New York: Bloomsbury T & T Clark, 2009), 109–21.

tion also indicated the beginning of a completely new messianic age. Jesus was not merely one more king in a long line of kings for Israel. He was the one who signaled that God was doing something entirely new and different. Paul expected nothing less from this new king than the eventual renewal of all of creation (Rom. 8:18–25). In fact, he believed that renewal had already begun, not only in the resurrection of Jesus but also in the assemblies of Jesus followers that Paul himself started. Those who responded to Paul's preaching had received the gift of the Holy Spirit, which Paul regarded as a sign of the new messianic age inaugurated by Jesus's resurrection (see Rom. 8:23; 1 Cor. 15:20; 2 Cor. 5:16–21; Gal. 3:1–4).

Paul's belief in this new age motivated his mission to non-Jews in the first place. Today, after two thousand years of predominantly gentile Christianity, it is easy to forget that Jesus and all of his first followers, including Paul, were devout Jews who believed in Jesus's very Jewish message about the kingdom of God. One could easily wonder how *any* non-Jews ever came to care about such a thoroughly Jewish phenomenon. For Paul, however, this was an exciting time for gentiles because it was finally the time in which they could join the kingdom of God *as* gentiles. They didn't have to become Jewish to become followers of Jesus precisely *because* Jesus had inaugurated this new messianic age in which even gentiles could be included (see Rom. 4:1–12; Gal. 3:1–28).

Nevertheless, Paul did expect significant changes from his gentile converts as they became new creatures themselves in this new age. We often see, in these ethical exhortations by Paul, that Paul's theology is actually quite political, even while his use of kingdom language is relatively rare. His theology is not political in the sense that he is encouraging the recipients of his letters to run for civic office. Rather, it is political in the sense that its central confession is "Jesus is Lord" (during a period of history when "lord" itself is a political title), and in that he is constantly encouraging his followers to conduct themselves as citizens of this new messianic kingdom rather than as part of the body politic of the Roman Empire.[9] Philippians 2:5–11 may be the most succinct summary of how Paul expects kingdom citizens to conduct themselves. Jesus—although being in the form

---

9. Phil. 1:27. The word translated as "conduct yourselves" or "live your life" in most translations of this verse is *politeuesthe*, which, like the English word "politic," has to do with conducting oneself as a citizen.

of God—did not grasp at power but repeatedly surrendered it for the good of others. For Paul, Christ's lordship consists precisely in his willingness to lay aside its corresponding power and privilege. Paul imitated this same pattern in his own ministry, believing that Christ's power was made perfect in weakness rather than strength, and he expected anyone who proclaimed Jesus as Lord to do the same (see 1 Cor. 4:11–13; 2 Cor. 4:7–12; 12:8–10; Phil. 3:4–8).

Jesus's Un-kingly Nature in the Gospels

Unlike Paul, the Gospels make use of kingdom language regularly. In fact, in the Gospel of Mark, Jesus's very first public words are, "The time is fulfilled, and the kingdom of God has come near" (1:15, NRSV). Introducing Jesus this way is most likely Mark's way of summarizing Jesus's central message—the main point of the sermons he preached over and over again throughout Judea. Throughout the Gospels, Jesus repeatedly elaborates on the nature of this kingdom through stories and parables. Furthermore, Jesus is portrayed as not only speaking this kingdom proclamation with words but also embodying it with actions—healing the sick, casting out demons, and attending to the poor and marginalized.[10]

A particularly telling episode regarding Jesus's kingly identity occurs in Mark 8:27–30. Jesus asks the disciples what others think about him. "Who do people say I am?" The disciples answer that some think he is John the Baptist or one of the prophets.[11] Jesus then turns the question to the disciples

---

10. In this section, I rely heavily on a single episode from Mark's Gospel that is fairly representative of the Gospels' depiction of Jesus's self-understanding as king. A more comprehensive treatment of the topic would give attention to the differences among the four Gospels' depictions of Jesus. Since such a treatment would require a much longer chapter, I have chosen to focus on Mark, which is understood as most likely being the earliest of the four Gospels and appears to provide a basic framework for Matthew and Luke. The following is not a comprehensive list, but even this brief accounting should be enough to indicate just how much kingdom language is the focus of the Gospels: Matt. 12:25–26/Mark 3:23–26/Luke 11:17–18; Matt. 13:11/Mark 4:11/Luke 8:10; Matt. 19:23/Mark 10:23/Luke 18:25; Matt. 26:29/Mark 15:43/Luke 22:16, 18; Matt. 20:21/Mark 10:37; Matt. 5:3/Luke 6:20; Matt. 6:33/Luke 12:31; Matt. 6:10/Luke 11:2; Matt. 8:11/Luke 13:28; Matt. 10:7/Luke 9:2; Matt. 13:33/Luke 13:20; Matt. 4:23; 5:10; 5:19; 7:21; 9:35; 13:1–52; 16:19; 18:23; Mark 4:26; 12:34; Luke 4:43; 8:1; 9:60–62; 10:9–11; 17:20–21; 21:31; 23:42.

11. It makes sense, historically speaking, that this is exactly how most people would have perceived Jesus in his lifetime. Jesus acts very much like the prophets of Israel; he

themselves: "But who do you say that I am?" Peter says, "You are the Messiah [Greek: *christos*]." As we've seen already, this assertion is very much in line with what Mark and the rest of the New Testament writers say about Jesus. In essence, Peter gets the right answer to Jesus's pop quiz.

However, immediately after Peter makes this confession, Jesus begins to talk about how he must suffer and die at the hands of the religious leaders in Jerusalem. Upon hearing this, Peter quickly takes Jesus aside and essentially says, "Hey, you've got to stop talking this way." (Most translations say Peter "rebuked" Jesus.) Peter has just confessed that Jesus is the Messiah, the Christ, the King of Israel. He has proclaimed Jesus as the one who will save his people, and now Jesus is talking about suffering. In Peter's mind, these two things cannot coexist. If Jesus is the Messiah, he cannot suffer. He is supposed to be the one to inflict suffering on the unrighteous sinners who have oppressed Israel. Jesus is to be the conquering hero, not the conquered one—and, therefore, a failure as a messiah. For Peter, his confession of Jesus as Messiah and Jesus's talk of suffering are mutually exclusive. What is more, Peter is so certain that he is right on this matter that he is willing to *rebuke* Jesus—his teacher, whom he has just proclaimed Messiah! Peter is confident that he can teach the Messiah a thing or two about what it means to be Messiah, and lesson number one is that a Messiah does *not* suffer.

Jesus's response to Peter's rebuke is about as strong as it possibly can be: "Get behind me, Satan!" (v. 33, NRSV). Why the harsh name-calling? Why does the kind and compassionate Jesus, who is so often the friend of sinners, equate one of his closest disciples with the evil one himself? Jesus says that Peter's mind is on human rather than divine things. Jesus goes on to say that anyone who wishes to become one of his followers must "deny themselves and take up their cross and follow me" (v. 34, NRSV).

It seems to me that the reason Jesus is so adamant on this point is that it cuts to the very heart of his understanding of his identity as Messiah and King. For Peter, messiah means winning. For Jesus, it means service, sacrifice, and suffering. This discussion is about the nature of Jesus's kingdom and its relationship with earthly power. Peter sees Jesus's kingdom as roughly like most other kingdoms—one established through the traditional means of power and dominance. The primary difference for Peter between

---

calls for justice for the poor and disenfranchised, he urges Israel to repent, and he enacts this message in unusual, symbolic actions (like turning over tables in the temple).

this kingdom and any other is who's in charge instead of the Romans—namely, Jesus, and the God of Israel. But Jesus has been trying to tell Peter and his other disciples just the opposite—that his kingdom is one that grows in secret, that it is like the tiniest of seeds that grows wildly and mysteriously, and that it belongs to those who have as much status in world politics as little children (Mark 4:26–27, 30–32; 10:13–16). Jesus's kingdom is meant to be completely unlike any other kingdom the world has ever known in that it is not predicated on power and influence but on love and sacrifice. This single point—the un-kingdom-like character of his kingdom—is so important to Jesus that he is willing to label anyone who misses the point as falling victim to the work of Satan.

In the verses immediately prior to this conversation between Jesus, Peter, and the other disciples, a blind man is brought to Jesus for healing. It's a rather odd story for a number of reasons, not least of which is that Jesus uses his spit to heal the man's eyes. It also appears strange at first glance because Jesus *fails* to heal the man on the first try. After touching the man, Jesus asks if he can see anything. The man responds that he can see people, "but they look like trees, walking" (8:24, NRSV). I can relate because this is more or less how the world appears to me without my glasses. The man has gained some sight, but his vision is far from clear. Jesus then touches the man again, and this time he is able to see everything clearly. Why was Jesus not able to heal the man on the first try? It seems that Mark has intentionally put this story of the man imperfectly healed in front of Peter's imperfect understanding of Messiah so that we might see the former as a metaphor for the latter. Peter sees who Jesus is—the Christ, God's anointed King—but his vision of what that *means* is imperfect. Peter's vision of Jesus's kingly identity is akin to seeing people as if they were trees walking around. Peter is in need of a second touch from Jesus so he can fully see that God's kingdom is a kingdom where the last will be first—one in which the meek, rather than the powerful, will inherit the earth (Mark 9:35; 10:31; Matt. 5:5). That is a very unusual kingdom with a very unusual king.

The primary aim of this chapter has been to offer an interpretation of the historical context in which Jesus and his followers proclaimed him as king. The other chapters in this section will provide a more in-depth theological conversation about what it means for current followers of Jesus to make that proclamation. I readily confess that I don't know all the specifics of what proclaiming Jesus as King means for those who wish to follow Jesus in the twenty-first century. Indeed, it will likely mean very different things in different contexts and communities. But I suspect, at the very least, it may mean this: *that, as followers of Jesus, one of the most central and critical tasks of our discipleship is to reflect at length and in depth on our relationship to power.* One of the most definitive qualities of the New Testament writers' witness to Jesus's kingly nature was to redefine the very nature of power and its role in Jesus's kingdom. It would seem that those who wish to be counted today as Jesus's followers should continue to do the same.

Suggestions for Further Reading

Arnold, Bill T., and H. G. M. Williamson, eds. *Dictionary of the Old Testament: Historical Books.* Downers Grove, IL: IVP Academic, 2005.

Baker, Mark D., and Joel B. Green. *Recovering the Scandal of the Cross: Atonement in New Testament and Contemporary Contexts.* Second edition. Downers Grove, IL: IVP Academic, 2011.

Bockmuehl, Markus, and James Carleton Paget, eds. *Redemption and Resistance: The Messianic Hopes of Jews and Christians in Antiquity.* New York: Bloomsbury T & T Clark, 2009.

Brueggemann, Walter. *Theology of the Old Testament: Testimony, Dispute, Advocacy.* Minneapolis: Fortress Press, 2012.

Levine, Amy-Jill. *The Misunderstood Jew: The Church and the Scandal of the Jewish Jesus.* New York: HarperOne, 2007.

Lucass, Shirley. *The Concept of the Messiah in the Scriptures of Judaism and Christianity.* New York: Bloomsbury T & T Clark, 2011.

Neusner, Jacob, William Scott Green, and Ernest S. Frerichs. *Judaisms and Their Messiahs at the Turn of the Christian Era.* New York: Cambridge University Press, 1987.

Novenson, Matthew V. *Christ among the Messiahs: Christ Language in Paul and Messiah Language in Ancient Judaism.* New York: Oxford University Press, 2012.

Wright, N. T. *Jesus and the Victory of God.* Vol. 1, *Christian Origins and the Question of God.* Minneapolis: Fortress Press, 1996.

10 ✝ FOLLOWING JESUS IN THE KINGDOM WAY

Mary K. Schmitt

THE GOSPEL of Mark may not explicitly call Jesus a king, but for those reading his account of Jesus and the kingdom he brings, there is no confusion about who he is.[1] Jesus is the king who is bringing a kingdom, and that kingdom has a *way*. In fact, Mark gives us a distinct understanding of the kingdom Jesus brings, by thematically using terminology that alludes to "the way of the Lord," a fascinating biblical motif that can help us understand the way of Jesus's kingdom.

In learning about the pattern of the kingdom Jesus brings, we are also challenged to join the way of that kingdom and walk in it. Built into the very notion that Jesus brings a kingdom identified as "the way of the Lord" is the implication that this way is to be walked and lived. This challenge, however, is no trivial matter. In Mark's Gospel, everything Jesus does and says along the way sets his kingdom in direct opposition to the authorities of this world so that they either must change their ways or crucify him. Those who choose to follow the ways of Jesus's kingdom may find themselves similarly in conflict with governing authorities today. And so we turn to Mark's Gospel, taking account not only of the distinctive kind of kingdom Jesus brings but also of how we might follow him as king into its distinct way.

---

1. Both Luke and John refer to Jesus as king in association with his entry into Jerusalem: "Blessed is the king who comes in the name of the Lord!" (Luke 19:38, NIV); "Blessed is the king of Israel!" (John 12:13, NIV).

The King Enters

In Mark 11, Jesus rode into Jerusalem seated on a donkey. The crowds spread their garments on the road, cut leafy branches, and shouted, "Hosanna! Blessed is the one who comes in the name of Lord! Blessed is the coming kingdom of our Father David! Hosanna in the highest!" (vv. 9–10).[2] We could easily think of the great king Solomon here, who rode a mule into Jerusalem when he was crowned king after his father, David (1 Kings 1:38). Jesus's choice of the donkey could also remind us of Zechariah's prophecy, which Matthew explicitly quotes: "See your king comes to you gentle and riding on a donkey" (Zech. 9:9; Matt. 21:5). None of this was lost on those who witnessed Jesus drawing near to the city. As he approached, the people cried out, "Blessed is the coming kingdom of our father David" (Mark 11:10, NIV).[3] Jesus, the son of David, rode into Jerusalem. The king entered.

The close relationship between King Jesus and the coming of the kingdom can be inferred from Jesus's first words in the Gospel of Mark: "The time has been fulfilled; the kingdom of God has drawn near" (1:15).[4] For Mark, the kingdom of God is not only a place but also a movement. It is advancing, breaking into the world through the words and actions of its king. Gladly for us, Mark employs a motif that helps us follow the in-breaking of the kingdom through the actions of the king. He writes about the "way of the Lord." From the opening lines of his Gospel, Mark alerts us to a kingdom movement, signaled in the prophetic command to "prepare the way of the Lord" (1:2–3). That pattern develops and continues throughout

---

2. Unless otherwise noted, all translations in this chapter are the author's own.

3. "Blessed is the one who comes in the name of the Lord" is a quotation from Psalm 118:26. James Sanders has argued that Psalm 118 is a royal coronation hymn. "A Hermeneutic Fabric: Psalm 118 in Luke's Entrance Narrative" in *Luke and Scripture*, eds. Craig A. Evans and James A. Sanders (Eugene, OR: Wipf and Stock, 1989). David Catchpole has compared this scene in Mark's Gospel with the arrival of other successful leaders, including Solomon, Judas Maccabeus, and others. The trope of successful leader entering the city and proceeding to the temple was familiar to Mark's first-century audience. "The 'Triumphal' Entry" in *Jesus and the Politics of His Day*, eds. E. Bammel and C. F. D. Moule (Cambridge: Cambridge University Press, 1984).

4. The two verbs in this sentence—*peplērōtai*, "has been fulfilled," and *ēngiken*, "has drawn near"—occur in the perfect tense in Greek. The perfect tense expresses a completed action with a continuing implication for the present. Often this verse is translated as "the kingdom is at hand." But Mark says the kingdom has come and is now near in the person of Jesus, the one proclaiming this message.

Mark's Gospel in his use of the Greek word *hodos*, which can be translated either "road" or "way" (1:2, 3; 2:23; 4:4, 15; 6:8; 8:3, 27; 9:33, 34; 10:17, 32, 46, 52; 11:8; 12:14). As Jesus approached Jerusalem, then, amidst the sounds of cheering crowds who welcomed him by spreading their garments "on the way," we should not miss this significant point: they were, quite literally, preparing the way of the Lord.[5] We should also not miss that "the way" in Mark leads to Jerusalem—the place where Jesus would ultimately be crucified; Mark also uses the motif of "the way" to refer to the manner of Jesus's life. These are the ways of the king and, by implication, the ways of his kingdom.

The Ways of the Kingdom

In Mark's Gospel, Jesus proclaimed the arrival of the kingdom of God, but descriptions of the kingdom remain elusive. Much like the parables, which compare the kingdom of God to everyday realities and offer glimpses of the characteristics of the kingdom, so too do the words and deeds of the king along the way offer glimpses into the nature of the kingdom. Just as with the parables, the picture of the kingdom is incomplete; these are merely glimpses of the kingdom, not its blueprint. Nevertheless, from the glimpses, one begins to get a sense of what this kingdom entails. The kingdom that is arriving with Jesus challenges assumptions about things like power, possessions, and individualism. While we cannot tease out every implication of the ways of Jesus's kingdom, at least four rise to our attention.

First, the way of the kingdom challenges and rejects consumerism. Following Jesus as king into the pattern of the kingdom he brings means refusing the captivating temptation to confuse needs with wants. This way exchanges a tight grip on excessive possessions for an open hand that holds possessions lightly. Mark tells us that Jesus addressed physical needs at several places along the way. After speaking all day, Jesus refused to send the crowd—numbering in the thousands—home hungry, afraid they would "faint on the way" (8:3). Taking account of the crowd's physical need and the meager provisions his disciples had with them, he fed the hungry crowds. Likewise, the first glimpse of the way of the kingdom occurred

---

5. See Joel Marcus, *The Way of the Lord* (Louisville: Westminster John Knox Press, 1992), 43.

on the Sabbath in Mark 2. The disciples were hungry and began to pluck heads of grain and to eat (v. 23). The Pharisees objected to this action on legal grounds, citing the prohibition against work on the Sabbath, but Jesus responded by recalling how David and his companions ate the bread that was solely reserved for priests when they were hungry. Jesus concluded, "So, the Son of Man is Lord of the Sabbath" (v. 28). There were two concerns here: what was lawful on the Sabbath and the disciples' hunger. Jesus addressed both by demonstrating that it was appropriate to provide for a person's physical needs on the Sabbath.[6] One's most basic needs are met in the kingdom of God.

There is, however, a difference between what one needs and what one wants. When Jesus sent pairs of disciples out to minister, he told them to take only a staff and sandals—not bread, nor a bag, nor money. He added that they were not to take two tunics (6:7–9). They were only to take what was necessary on the way. The contrast between needs and wants can be found in Exodus as well. In a manna economy, Israelites were instructed to take only what they needed for each day (Exod. 16:1–36; Num. 11:1–9). In contrast, Pharaoh's economy involved building larger storehouses to hold all his possessions (Exod. 1:11). The kingdom of God in Mark was similar to the manna economy in Exodus: one took only the necessities.[7]

A kingdom of limited possessions stands in contrast to a consumerist economy like Pharaoh's. In a consumerist economy, one can never have enough. Holding tightly to possessions begins to control decision-making, even potentially closing off the possibility for one to walk in the way of the kingdom Jesus was bringing. Jesus, in Mark's Gospel, noted that calling for limited possessions was a barrier to some potential disciples. In response to a man who asked Jesus what he should do to inherit eternal life, Jesus said to sell all his possessions and give to the poor in order to have treasure in heaven. Mark reports that the man went away sad because "he had many possessions" (10:22). Jesus twice expressed to his disciples how difficult it would be for those who had many possessions or much wealth to enter the kingdom of God (10:23, 25). Excessive possessions become a burden along the way; thus, the king invites his followers to be free from the control of consumerism and to take only what they need on the journey.

---

6. C. Clifton Black, *Mark* (Nashville: Abingdon, 2011), 97–98.
7. Joel Marcus, *Mark 1–8* (New York: Doubleday, 2000), 389.

The day after Jesus entered Jerusalem to the delighted welcome of the people, he returned to the city and went to the temple. There, he found the temple courts filled with people buying and selling goods. He overturned the tables of the moneychangers, drove out those selling doves, and refused to allow anyone to carry merchandise through the temple (11:15–16).[8] Jesus's words were an indictment of the temple authorities: the temple should be a "house of prayer for all nations. But *you* have made it a hideout for robbers" (v. 17, emphasis added).[9] Jesus's charge of economic misappropriation issued an uncomfortable challenge to the chief priest and scribes, who immediately began searching for a way to destroy him. They opted to crucify him rather than give up the financial benefits of the current system (v. 18).[10] A few chapters later, the same chief priests and scribes were still looking for a way to arrest Jesus when Judas approached them and asked for money (14:10).[11] He colluded with the authorities in exchange for personal financial benefit, joining the way of the authorities and turning away from the way of Jesus. In passages like this, we see that walking the way of the kingdom of God challenges narratives of personal consumerism. When confronted with the selfishness of such narratives, it seems easier to crucify Jesus than to give up our possessions and the status quo. Nevertheless, in giving up everything, including his own life, Jesus showed that being controlled by one's possessions or the allure of wealth was not the way of the kingdom of God.

---

8. This event is sometimes mistakenly referred to as the temple cleansing. After Antiochus Epiphanes defiled the temple in 164 BCE, the temple had to be cleansed. See Kent Brower, *Mark: A Commentary in the Wesleyan Tradition* (Kansas City: Beacon Hill Press of Kansas City, 2012).

9. The Greek word *humeis*, which is the plural you ("y'all"), is added for emphasis.

10. The Greek word *lēstēs*, translated here as "robbers," is typically the word used for bandits or brigands. The Jewish historian Josephus used this word to refer to revolutionaries during the Jewish Revolt (e.g., *Jewish Antiquities* 14.15; 15.10; *Jewish War* 1.16). That usage is probably intended here, but an economic charge is also implied. The accusation is violent extortion of people's money. See Joel Marcus, *Mark 8–16* (New Haven, CT: Yale University Press, 2009), 784.

11. Judas, along with the other disciples, just watched a woman waste a jar of expensive perfume by dumping it on Jesus's feet. Indignant, the disciples asked why the perfume was not sold and the money given to the poor (Mark 14:4–5). John's Gospel explains that Judas was particularly indignant because he, the treasurer, had been stealing from the collective moneybox (12:6).

Second, the way of the kingdom introduces a new way of sharing life together. The way of Jesus is not a way to be walked in solitude but one that draws us into vital relationship with one another. We see this prominently in Jesus's choice to select twelve disciples to accompany him on the way.[12] When he sent the disciples out, he sent them in pairs, revealing the necessity of community for the kingdom of God (6:7).[13] This is not a kingdom of individuals. The subjects of this kingdom are called to live and minister together. Moreover, part of the reason the disciples did not have to take possessions with them on the way is that they could rely on the resources of the community. Jesus told the disciples that, in every town, they were to enter a house and stay there until they left the town. If anyone refused them, they were to shake the dust off their feet as a witness against them (6:10–11). The expectation was that the community would provide.

Interestingly, in Mark, the authorities were reluctant to arrest Jesus because of the people he had gathered (e.g., 11:18; 12:12; 14:2). Repeatedly, Mark mentions that the crowds were amazed by Jesus and by his teaching (1:22; 6:2, 7:37; 10:26).[14] The authorities recognized that Jesus's message would shift power and authority away from them; thus, they sought to put an end to the message bearer. Fearing a riot among the people, though, the chief priests and scribes tried to arrest Jesus secretly and kill him (14:1–2). When they *did* arrest him, Jesus noted that he had taught publicly every day in the temple courts—yet they chose to arrest him in the privacy of the garden of Gethsemane (v. 49).

At the moment of his arrest, all the disciples left Jesus and fled (v. 50). The desertion of the disciples differs from the rest of the Gospel, in which the overwhelming presence of crowds often kept Jesus out of cities (1:45; 2:4; 3:20; 4:1). The isolation of that moment reflects the brokenness of the world, which is confronted by a God who seeks to overcome brokenness and isolation. After the resurrection, the women were instructed to tell the

---

12. Mark explicitly explains Jesus's rationale in calling the Twelve as fellowship: "in order that they might be with him" (3:14).

13. The practice of going out in pairs is attested to in Judaism (e.g., *b Sanh* 26a and 43a) and continues in the early church as described in Acts 8:14; 13:2; and 15:2. See Marcus, *Mark 1–8*, 383; Brower, *Mark*, 168.

14. Joel Marcus (*Mark 8–16*, 784) notes that the Greek word ἐκπλήσσω (*ekplēssō*) literally means "overwhelmed." So the crowds may not have necessarily agreed with Jesus or his teachings, but they recognized his authority.

disciples to gather in Galilee (16:7). The kingdom of God restores community; this is not a collection of individuals but a reconciled people of God.

Third, the way of this kingdom opens a new way to discern the pattern of leadership. On the way to Capernaum, the disciples learned about servant leadership in the kingdom of God. They had been discussing among themselves who was greatest. Their discussion revealed that they did not yet understand the nature of Jesus's kingdom.[15] In response, Jesus declared, "The one who wants to be first will be last of all and a servant of all" (9:35). Jesus deemed the least to be the most important in the kingdom of God. Similarly, Jesus insisted that the kingdom of heaven belonged to children (10:15). This claim that one must become like a child to enter the kingdom was followed by the insistence that it is difficult for the wealthy to enter the kingdom of God (vv. 23, 25). Most kingdoms of the earth are ruled by the powerful and wealthy. But Jesus's kingdom is revealed along the way as a kingdom of the least of these—a kingdom of servants and children.

In the verses immediately preceding the disciples' argument over who is greatest, Jesus predicted his own death and resurrection: "Jesus was teaching his disciples, saying, 'The Son of Man will be handed over into human hands, and they will kill him, and three days after dying he will be raised.' But they did not understand the claim, and they were afraid to ask him" (9:31–32). Their debate about who was greatest underscored the extent to which they misunderstood. The Son of Man's leadership was demonstrated by giving up his life. Jesus's prophecy of his death and resurrection beforehand, which he does in each Gospel, is referred to by the shorthand phrase "passion prediction."[16] The passion prediction in 9:31–32 is the second of three in Mark's Gospel (8:31–32; 9:31–32; 10:33–34)—and, fascinatingly, the whole section is framed by two references to "the way" of the Lord (9:27; 10:52).[17]

In Mark 8:27, Jesus was walking with the disciples on the way to Caesarea Philippi when he asked them, "Who do people say I am?"

They replied, "John the Baptist," "Elijah," or "one of the prophets."

---

15. In response to Jesus asking what they were discussing on the way, the disciples said nothing. Brower notes that their silence "implies that they are aware of the dissonance between their debate and Jesus' teaching . . . Their discussion shows that their way is not the way of the Lord." *Mark*, 254–55.

16. Matt. 16:21–28; Luke 9:22–27; John 8:27–30.

17. Werner H. Kelber, *The Kingdom in Mark: A New Place and a New Time* (Philadelphia: Fortress Press, 1974).

Then he asked, "But you, who do you say I am?"

Peter correctly confessed, "You are the Christ."

But when Jesus immediately began the first passion prediction (v. 31), Peter rejected this as the role of the Messiah (v. 32). From Peter's perspective, the Christ came to conquer, not to be killed. A suffering Messiah did not fit the disciples' notion of leadership, but leadership in the kingdom of God looks like service.

The third passion prediction also occurred along the way. Walking toward Jerusalem, Jesus again predicted his death (10:33–34), and the disciples again demonstrated that they did not understand leadership in the kingdom of God. James and John came to Jesus and asked to sit on his right and on his left in his coming kingdom (v. 37). Jesus responded that the places of honor in his kingdom were reserved for those able "to drink the cup I drink and to be baptized in the baptism in which I am baptized" (v. 38).[18] Jesus's reference to the cup he would drink calls to mind the scene from the garden of Gethsemane, where he prayed that the cup of suffering might pass from him (14:36). To drink the cup Jesus drank is to be prepared to suffer the way Jesus suffered. James and John did not yet understand this, but Jesus implied that they would—which was, perhaps, a reference to their eventual martyrdoms and deaths (10:39).

James and John were not alone in their misunderstanding; the other ten disciples were indignant when they heard about the brothers' request because they wanted to be in positions of leadership as well. But Jesus once again explained that the world's views of leadership and power were not the way of the kingdom of God: "You know that the so-called rulers of the world lord power over their constituents . . . but thus it is not among you. Whoever wants to be great among you will be your servant and whoever wants to be first will be slave of all. For even the Son of Man did not come to be served, but to serve and to give his life as a ransom on behalf of all" (10:42–45). Jesus contrasted worldly leaders who abused their positions of power with leadership in the kingdom of the God. To be a leader in the

---

18. Interestingly, Jesus's response invokes the sacraments of Eucharist and baptism. At the Last Supper in Mark, Jesus takes the cup, which is the covenant of his blood poured out for many (14:24). Moreover, he claims he will not drink from the cup again until he drinks anew in the kingdom of God (v. 25). Perhaps Mark suggests that we enter the kingdom through the practice of the sacraments. See also Black, *Mark*, 232.

---

kingdom of God is counterintuitive; it involves giving up power and serving the other.

This message of servant leadership did not sit well with the leaders of Jesus's time. One of the key questions surrounding Jesus, as Mark's Gospel tells it, was by what authority he acted and spoke (e.g., 2:10, 11:28). The crowds from the beginning described Jesus as one who taught with authority in contrast to the scribes (1:22, 27). After the triumphal entry and the temple incident, the chief priests, the scribes, and the elders again asked Jesus by whose authority he did such things (11:28). He did not answer them directly but told a parable about a man who planted a vineyard and left it in the care of some tenants (12:1–11). At the time of the harvest, the tenants beat the servants who came to collect the owner's dues. Finally, the vineyard owner sent his son, whom the tenants killed. Jesus insisted that, because of their actions, the keepers of the vineyard would be replaced. The authorities of Jesus's day knew that he spoke the parable against them, and they sought to arrest him (v. 12). They had been appointed as servants of the vineyard, yet Jesus foretold that, rather than give up their authority, they would kill him. The servant leadership of the kingdom of God posed a challenge to the authorities of their world; those who refuse to give up their power have no option other than to destroy the one calling for a reversal of power dynamics.

Fourth, the way of this kingdom often means coming into conflict with those who may oppose the kind of kingdom Jesus brings. The way in Mark is by no means safe. The kingdom is under attack by other powers that are threatened by the seedling potential of the message. Mark not only admits that the kingdom will not take root in some places, but he also insists that other powers may actively seek to prevent the kingdom of God from being established (4:4). Those in power do not want to give up their places of authority; the stockpiling of material goods does not make space for newness and growth.

In a memorable passage from Mark, Jesus told a parable about a farmer who went out to sow seed, and some of the seed fell along the road/way (hodos) and was devoured by birds (4:4). When the disciples asked Jesus to explain the parable, he equated the birds with Satan, who he said comes and takes away the sown word (v. 15). Since they occur within a parable, it might be easy to overlook these references to "the way." Yet, given the significance of the motif we are exploring in Mark, it seems likely that the term appears intentionally, a reminder that opposition should not be a surprise to one who walks the way of Jesus's kingdom. The ultimate form of opposition, of course, is the death of the one who faithfully walks the way, but Jesus did not shy away from that possibility. The parable he told foreshadowed the role of the authorities in Mark's crucifixion scene. They sought to stop this movement before it got out of hand by subjecting Jesus to crucifixion; but even their best attempts did not stop the flourishing of the kingdom Jesus brought.

Examining Jesus's deeds and actions along "the way" in Mark's Gospel has highlighted the way that Jesus's actions and commands put the kingdom community in the crosshairs of other governing powers. The world's ways—of climbing over anyone and everyone, trying to accumulate as much as possible to keep for one's individual use—are exposed in the light of the ways of the kingdom of God. When the tension between the kingdom of God and other kingdoms becomes too great, human authorities will feel they have no option other than to put to death the leader of the new kingdom.

The King on the Cross

When we read a passage like Mark 11 and see the images of rapturous crowds cheering the arrival of one who takes on kingly symbols that are similar to those of the greatest kings in Jewish history, we might expect the story to conclude with a coronation. In Mark, Jesus is enthroned, but a perverse kind of coronation puts him on a cross rather than in a palace, and then we see a profound shift in the way Mark speaks about Jesus. While, up to this point, Mark has been reluctant to use the word "king" to describe Jesus, in the passion narrative Jesus is called king five times.[19] Pilate asked Jesus if he was the "king of the Jews" (15:2). His question paralleled that of the high priest, who earlier asked Jesus if he was "the Christ" (14:61). Ironically, both religious and political leaders correctly named Jesus as king. According to Mark, Pilate even offered to release the "king of the Jews" (15:9), but the chief priests stirred up the crowds to request the release of the murderer Barabbas instead (v. 11). The crowd insisted that the king of the Jews be crucified. Thus began the perverse coronation.

19. Frank J. Matera, *The Kingship of Jesus: Composition and Theology in Mark 15* (Chico, CA: Scholars Press, 1982), 157–59.

The soldiers dressed Jesus in a royal-purple robe and placed a crown of thorns on his head. They knelt, even bowed, before him, crying out, "Hail, King of the Jews!" (vv. 17–19). They mockingly enacted the ritual of coronation, though the actual ascension was to a cross instead of a throne. When he was lifted up, a sign was placed above Jesus's head, again identifying him as "The King of the Jews" (v. 26). The chief priest and scribes mocked him further, saying, "The Christ, the King of Israel—let him come down now from the cross in order that we might see it and believe" (v. 32). Of course, the King of Israel *had* come down, had become incarnate, but they had not believed. Instead, they crucified him.

To anyone following along with Mark's narrative, the cross does not come as a surprise. Jesus predicted his death three times along the way. Even more than the explicit predictions, his actions and words continually placed him in direct conflict with human authorities. Since the earliest days of his ministry, the authorities had sought to kill him because he proclaimed a kingdom at odds with the values of the world (3:6). He challenged their authority by exposing economic disparities. He uncovered the lack of inclusion in positions of leadership. And he did all of this while proclaiming that his way was the way of the kingdom of God. Those listening must either respond by joining him along the way or by trying to put an end to his journey.

Following the Way of the King

There is one other mention of "the way" in Mark's Gospel. The Pharisees and Herodians approached Jesus and asked him a question, trying to trap him in his words. "You teach *the way* of God according to the truth. Is it acceptable to pay taxes to Caesar or not?" (12:13–14, emphasis added). These religious and political leaders were bluntly asking Jesus if the ways of the kingdom of God were the same as the ways of another king, Caesar. Jesus asked them to show him a denarius—a coin worth a day's wages. Both the image and the inscription, which read, "Tiberius Caesar Augustus, son of the deified Augustus," reinforced that Caesar was king of the Roman Empire.[20] Caesar's kingdom was tied to money, power, and his individual personhood. When the leaders asked Jesus if the kingdom of God was the

---

20. Marcus, *Mark 8–16*, 824.

same kind of kingdom as Caesar's, those who had been following Jesus on the way knew the answer was a resounding no.

Jesus responded, "Give to Caesar the things belonging to Caesar, and to God the things belonging to God" (12:17). This reply, often interpreted as a neutral response to political governments, was actually a biting criticism of those authorities who had just asked the question.[21] The question itself suggested that these leaders had bought into Caesar's kingdom of money and power. However, God's ways and Caesar's ways are different, and to choose the kingdom of God is not to choose the ways of the kingdoms of this world.

This episode between Jesus and the authorities points to the reality that we have been exploring: seeing Jesus as king, and following his ways, defies conventional logic and likely sets up opposition from those who do not recognize Jesus's kingdom. The ways of the kingdom of God challenge the values of other kingdoms. It is not possible to follow the kingdom of God and Caesar's kingdom at the same time. The paths diverge. To follow Jesus on the way is to reject all other kings and kingdoms—which, of course, comes with a risk. We know where the Lord's way took him. To follow the way of the kingdom of God is to lead a life that may result in similar persecutions from human authorities, but even in the face of that reality, it is still the way of Jesus.

---

21. This encounter immediately follows the parable of the wicked tenants (Mark 12:1–12). Jesus's response reinforces the charge that those who have been entrusted in Israel are not giving God (the owner of the vineyard) God's due. Brower, *Mark*, 311.

---

11 ✝ FOLLOWING JESUS IN CAESAR'S PRESENCE

Timothy L. P. Hahn

The Problem of Caesar

We all live somewhere. We all live some*when*. Although these realities are obvious, it is important to acknowledge them when we ask what it means that Jesus is King. On the one hand, the crucified Jew from Nazareth whom we confess as King also lived somewhere and somewhen. On the other hand, that same crucified Jew also lives *here* and *now*. The kingship of Jesus has present and concrete consequences. Moreover, our crucified King rules *there* and *then*. The kingdom of God—the kingdom where and when Christ is King—is a reality that has already been established—but is still being made complete. As much as it is pressingly and powerfully present, it is also promisingly and often frustratingly future.

So Jesus is King *then* and *there*, and he is King *here* and *now*. We, however, are bound to just the here and now, which presents a problem: however universal and complete the coming kingdom may be, we live our lives in a world where Jesus is not the only one who claims the authority to rule. We find ourselves unavoidably entangled in other political realities, other systems of government, other kingdoms, other empires.

Jesus is King, but we live in a world of Caesars.

This tension can be seen even in the Gospel accounts. Most of us have encountered the response of Jesus to the Pharisees and Herodians who, seeking to trap him, asked about the lawfulness of paying taxes to the emperor: "Give to the emperor the things that are the emperor's, and to God the things that are God's" (Matt. 22:21; Mark 12:17; Luke 20:25, all NRSV). Many of us will have heard such references used to "answer" the question of following Jesus as King while remaining in a world ruled by Caesars.

Even as Jesus stands trial before Pilate, we hear from his own mouth: "You would have no power over me unless it had been given you from above" (John 19:11, NRSV). Yet, elsewhere in the Gospel texts, and later in the New Testament as well, we see the reign of God—the kingship of Jesus—set over and against the powers of this world. Consider Mary's Magnificat in Luke 1:46–55; the contrast of citizenship in Philippians 3:20; and the subversive political imagery throughout Revelation.

Whatever may be made of these passages, for our purposes here, we should note that the New Testament witness does not resolve the dissonance brought by the confession of Jesus as King amidst the ongoing reality of Caesar's presence. The attempt to square this circle, if not made immediately clear by the New Testament witness alone, is a task of the imagination—by which I mean how we envision the possibility of living in certain ways, including the practices and concepts we use to realize that vision. In the context of political questions concerning Jesus's kingship and the persistence of Caesar's rule, this envisioning is called our *theopolitical imagination*. This terminology focuses on the relationship between our imagination—the vision, practices, and concepts by which we orient our life—and the theological and political demands of the gospel.

Before we can go much further, an important commitment should be made. Political language begets political imagery. Political communities tend to reflect the shape and nature of their ruler(s). Kings rule over kingdoms, governments govern their respective nations, and politics involve a body of political agents. This understanding is especially important when we consider the body that corresponds to Jesus our King. When we speak of the political implications of King Jesus, we necessarily speak about the *church*. The church is what we have in mind in this chapter when we use the word "we." Further, we should recognize that any talk of Christians imagined apart from the church is, at best, a demographic designation, and does not share in the theological language of the gospel. To speak of Christians is to speak of the citizens of that odd "city," the church. We are faced, then, with an unavoidable confrontation between two political realms, each necessarily shaped by the nature and character of its respective ruler(s).

It is important to note that we are not trying to present a vision of the kind of relationship the church should have with the state. Building a political theology on the kind of relationship the church should have with the state risks forming a theopolitical imagination in which Jesus and Caesar are somehow equal, but the kingship of Jesus requires something more. The kingship of Jesus requires that we stubbornly reserve that central position for Christ and Christ alone. That we must do so, however, is best explained in the sorts of arguments you will find in the other chapters of this book: those that deal explicitly with the meanings of Scripture and the consequences of Jesus's incarnation, life, death, and resurrection. Jesus is King, and this truth is of profound political importance, reaching far beyond the questions of church and state.

Over the last two thousand years, Christians' theopolitical imaginations have taken many and various forms. This chapter will present and analyze three of those forms. Each has an important lesson to teach us, and each also has an unacceptable consequence that should urge us to reject all three as ultimately unfaithful. In their place, I will offer some characteristics of what I pray is a faithful theopolitical imagination, a way to follow Jesus in Caesar's presence.

Three (Unsatisfactory) Options

Constantinianism: Idolatrous Identification

The first three centuries of the church were ones of intermittent persecution from the Roman Empire, which was the dominant political authority of the ancient Mediterranean. The Edict of Toleration in CE 311 ended the last, official, imperial persecution of Christians, and the Edict of Milan in CE 313 legalized the practice of Christianity. Constantine, labeled by history the first Christian emperor, issued these edicts, beginning a story that demonstrates our first example of theopolitical imagination. The sudden change of fortunes for the church in relation to the empire began an increasing tendency within the church to see the fulfillment of Jesus's kingship in the dominance of a Christian ruler. Constantinianism describes an imagination that developed over many centuries and involved multiple interpretations. For our purposes, however, Constantinianism involves associating the authority of Jesus our King with that of another political order.

This equation is not restricted to the ancient Roman world or to medieval Europe. Many American Christians today believe that the U.S. election results reveal the will of God. The United States is still thought of as a city on a hill, the world's only indispensable nation. Think of the ubiquity of American flags in church sanctuaries and the celebration of U.S. national holidays in Sunday worship. Think also of the ways in which many Christians associate a particular political party with Christianity. Think of the rhetoric that is employed, suggesting that the victory of one or another political party will "bring the nation back to God," or that a single, partisan issue—abortion or universal healthcare, for example—determines, on its own, whether a certain politic is or is not Christian. In the Constantinian imagination, the faithful Christian is identical to the ideal citizen; the pastor is a civil servant who perpetuates the state's wishes; and any potential for Christians to challenge the actions of the state are swallowed up in the conflation of Jesus with present political power. Here, Jesus is King, so the king must be Jesus.

Constantinianism has been appealing to so many for so long because it holds tightly to the *already* aspect of the kingdom initiated by Jesus and still awaiting fulfillment (Jesus's eschatological kingship, to use the technical term). The presentness of Christ's rule means that current political realities are the fabric of the kingdom of God. Scriptural commands to "seek the welfare of the city" (Jer. 29:7, NRSV) and to submit to authorities "instituted by God" (Rom. 13:1, NRSV) seem to support the Constantinian imagination, refusing an irresponsible neglect of political realities.

However, significant problems remain. If Jesus is King and so the king must be Jesus, we ought to immediately recognize the propensity of the Constantinian imagination to result in idolatry. In our zeal to realize the rule of Jesus our King, we can leave behind the Jesus witnessed to in Scripture and take instead our present king, our nation, our political party—our Caesar—as the definition of faithfulness. Political participation in nation or party takes on the mantle of Christian worship and witness. Political figures take on the mantle of Messiah. And the agents of the state—such as the military, for instance—take on the mantle of martyr.

Gnosticism: Artificial Separation

Whereas Constantinianism conflates the rule of Jesus with present political power, our second example of theopolitical imagination moves radically in the opposite direction. Gnosticism is a broad term that refers to a number of early Christian heresies that held in common the belief in a sharp division between the spiritual and the physical, between the divine and the material. The spiritual—and, thus, the strictly immaterial—was that which is "good" and capable of salvation. The physical was irredeemable, and salvation meant escaping the body and leaving behind the material world.

A Gnostic imagination insists on a sharp distinction between the spiritual and the physical. Translated into theopolitical terms, Gnostic ideology results in a disregard for political matters on the grounds of their unimportance in relation to the spiritual. We can see this imagination at work when Christians want to emphasize the care of the soul over and against the care of the body, or when political efforts for justice are ignored for the sake of "winning souls." A Gnostic imagination is evident when faith leaders are told to cease commenting on political issues and "stick to theology." Here, Jesus is King of our hearts and souls, and nothing else matters.

The strength of the Gnostic imagination is its refusal to fall into the trap of Constantinianism. When nothing earthly has value, there is little chance of the state displacing Jesus as the object of our worship. Equipped with this imagination, Christians might better avoid the vicious cycle of partisan hatred that currently characterizes most political discourse in our world—but Gnosticism ends up embracing idolatry in a different way. Its purely spiritual Jesus and his immaterial kingdom fail to take seriously the incarnation, the *fleshly*—and thus political—life of Jesus. Further, such an imagination fails to adequately consider the resurrection. The Gospels present to us a risen Jesus who *has a body*, for all its apparent difference from our own (see Luke 24:36–43; John 20:24–29). The Gnostic imagination sacrifices an embodied salvation for the sake of spiritualism and, in so doing, often ignores the all-too fleshly cries of the oppressed and suffering.

Post-liberalism: Necessary Opposition

Throughout the church's history, and increasingly in the last century, there have been Christians who recognize a dangerous combination of Constantinianism and Gnosticism. This combination generally encourages a Gnostic self-identity for the church, one in which religion is restricted to the inner lives of individuals. At the same time, the combination stresses the importance of the state, expressed primarily in the language of *national identity, patriotism,* and *civic responsibility*. The idolatry of the state that we see in Constantinianism is combined with a Gnostic neglect of public engagement by a church concerned only with inner things. The result is a church with divided loyalties: ignoring the political demands of the kingship of Jesus while failing to recognize their being co-opted into idolatry in service to the state.

In response to this combination we find the Post-liberal imagination, which insists on seeing the state through a theological lens while seeing the church through a political lens. It refuses the combination of Constantinianism and Gnosticism and combines the critiques of those positions. Understandably, the political weight of the church is highlighted in this approach, but it is often set up in necessary opposition to the state. Here, Jesus is King, and no other political reality matters.

I confess that, of the three imaginations discussed, I am most sympathetic to the Post-liberal line of thought. It applies rigorous and careful critiques to Constantinian political idolatry, *and* it rebuffs the Gnostic impulse toward escapism. It emphasizes the church as the locus of faithful Christian politics. But here too there is at least the possibility for problems. A Post-liberal imagination can encourage a sort of sectarianism in which the church becomes the only political space that matters, resulting in an effectively Gnostic neglect of the world.[1]

A Christomorphic Imagination

So what is to be done? The approaches outlined above are quite clearly present in various forms and mixtures today. Is there any way forward? How can we follow Jesus in the presence of other political systems, systems we cannot avoid? What is a Christian to do? How can a pastor faithfully lead a congregation?

I wish I could lay out a clear set of guidelines or a how-to plan for faithfully following Jesus as King in the presence of other political systems. If only we could choose one of the options considered above as best. Unfortunately, no such set of easy answers exists. As we have noted throughout, all such attempts to navigate this confrontation are efforts of imagination. In the place of the options outlined above, however, I want to suggest a Christomorphic[2] imagination. By "Christomorphic" I mean "having the form, or shape, of Christ" (from the Greek for "form" or "appearance," *morphē*).

---

1. Stanley Hauerwas and John Howard Yoder have responded to the charge of sectarianism with robust, political interpretations of "mission."

2. I borrow this term from Sarah Coakley's *God, Sexuality, and the Self: An Essay 'On the Trinity'* (Cambridge: Cambridge University Press, 2013).

When we seek the shape of our theopolitical imaginations, we are to look to Jesus. While this may suggest many different characteristics, here we will highlight three.

Scandalously Particular

To speak of Jesus is to speak of his particularity (see chapter 1). His ministry, death, and resurrection all participate in that particularity. Part of the power of the Christian gospel is the scandalous claim that this particular person—a poor Jew who lived and died in an imperial backwater along the eastern coast of the Mediterranean Sea two thousand years ago—is of cosmic significance. The ordering of particularity and universality is important. Jesus lived a concrete life in a concrete place. It is by the power of the Holy Spirit that his singular existence takes on universal scope.

Our imaginations ought to reflect this ordering. We do not deny that the political consequences of following Jesus as King have wide-ranging—in fact, universal—significance. But any attempt to follow Jesus faithfully, to shape (*morphoō*) our imagination and, thus, our life, must begin in a concrete time and a concrete place. It must be scandalously particular. Christians with a Christomorphic imagination are those who believe that gathering together for worship on a Sunday morning, or sharing a meal with their neighbors, or praying for a coworker are political acts that have cosmic implications. The Christomorphic imagination is embodied by the pastors whose sermons touch upon the issues of the communities where their parishioners live, who show up to the local high school theater production to laugh and cry with the people around them, who learn the names of the baristas who work at the local coffee shop. A scandalously particular imagination leads us to recognize that faithful political action has more to do with providing for the education of the children in our neighborhoods than with supporting a party platform. It has more to do with caring for the park down the street than with the election of government officials. It has more to do with concern for our neighbors than with the use of this or that hashtag.

Following Jesus in such scandalously particular fashion does not mean we imagine ourselves excused from the large-scale realities of our unavoidably political existence. But it does lean in to faith in the power of the Holy Spirit. By this Spirit the absurdly local acts of sharing meals, praying, knowing names, being present, caring for children, cleaning parks, building community, and—perhaps most especially—congregational worship are incorporated into the cosmic reign of Jesus, who is our King. By the power of the Holy Spirit, the particular can become the universal. Economic justice may be embraced, refugee crises may be resolved, escalating violence and threats of violence may be pacified, ecological disaster may be redeemed, fragmented lives may be healed, and idolatry and hatred may be defeated. The global scale of our political needs find their answer in the particular body and life of Jesus Christ—which is to say the particular bodies and lives of the church—raised ever and always to new, universal life.

Stubbornly Theological

To speak of Jesus is to speak of God. And to speak of God is, literally, to speak theologically. Some assume that theology is only that sort of speech undertaken by specialists (theologians and pastors) and that whatever it is nonspecialists do when they talk about God, it is not theology. This is to sell short both the nonspecialist and the God of whom theology seeks to speak. For the God who is revealed in Jesus our King is the God who covenanted with the childless wanderer Abram, who chose the Israelites while they were a small and insignificant people of the ancient Levant, who promised a future to exiles crushed by empire, who partnered with a teenage virgin in Nazareth, who called apostles from fishermen and tax collectors, whose empty tomb was first proclaimed by women, who was shown forth in broken bread and shared cup, who comes to us in victory as the slaughtered Lamb, who is near to the weak and brokenhearted. God does not reserve Godself to specialists.

It should not surprise us, then, that the church's political language must also be theological language. We do not cease to do theology when we begin to engage politically. We are, however, often tempted to seek another route. Theological claims—because they assume the faith of the believer—are often incomprehensible in a pluralistic world. Because theological language can be so alien, the church often seeks to express itself in other language. Sometimes the church seeks to frame itself as a sort of Constantinian power bloc. The church's political life is understood in terms of its impact on elections or as a source of campaign donations. In these instances, the church's political witness is expressed in a language of domination that is quite at odds with the crucified Jew we claim as our King. At other times the church frames its political life as an effort to support and extend a specific moral framework. Disembodied ethical arguments are put forward as the content of the church's political witness, ignoring the fact that—disconnected from the story of Jesus and the communities who practice his particular way—these ethical arguments make little sense. Not only is the moralizing political message of today's Christians strangely selective in the choice of issues deemed nonnegotiable, but it also serves as yet another rhetorical weapon in a political battle to establish an all-too-earthly rule.

In the place of these inadequate modes of political expression, the church must be stubbornly theological. Our political language and our political actions *are* the means by which we speak of Jesus, who is our King, and vice versa. Speaking of Jesus our King *is* to speak and live politically—which means that the imaginative center of our language and life is none other than Jesus. Our political life is measured against his life, death, and resurrection.

Do our politics seek to dominate and subdue those we might imagine to be our enemies? Does our political witness find expression in forms that sling violence and hatred in the interest of acquiring power and influence? If so, we must confess that we have been shaped by "the course of this world, following the ruler of the power of the air" (Eph. 2:2, NRSV). The Christians whose imaginations are stubbornly theological will recognize that winning and losing elections has very little to do with following the King whose victory lay along the path of crucifixion and death. They will find their political voice in confessing the creed and praying the Lord's Prayer, rather than in the voting booths or the poll results. Pastors whose imaginations are stubbornly theological will recognize that their sermons, and not bitter Facebook posts, their celebration at the Lord's Table, and not sharp-tongued Tweets, are the way to guide the faithful along the way of Jesus the King. Or it may be that Facebook posts that point to Jesus, our crucified and risen King, rather than bitter sermons, a gentle Tweet, rather than a fenced Table, hold stubbornly to the theological center of a Christomorphic imagination.

Terrifyingly Pneumatological

To speak of Jesus is to speak by the Spirit. Here, finally, we confront a most difficult characteristic of following Jesus as King. Just as we have held together speaking and living in the preceding sections, so must we hold them together here. To follow Jesus as King is to live by the Spirit.

Statements like this are an integral part of our common Christian language, particularly in Wesleyan-Holiness traditions. Thus, we might initially fail to recognize its significance for our theopolitical imagination. In our world, politics is about *life*; it is about the securing of a future for some group of people, a city, a state, or a nation—which is part of why political conflict is often so bitter. At issue is the *how* and, often, the *whether* of life. How will a people's resources be allocated? What vital services will be provided and to whom? How will the people respond to threat? In the face of uncertainty, the political task for the kingdoms of this world—for Caesar—is to secure the future. Whether a political slogan is about making something what it once was (thus claiming to be grounded in an imagined past), or moving forward, or having hope, all politics are future-oriented.

Within this context, the claim that to follow Jesus as King is to live by the Spirit takes on a more strident meaning. The church that has a Christomorphic imagination follows the Jesus who became incarnate, lived, taught, and healed by the power of the Holy Spirit. This Jesus was led (or driven) into the wilderness *by the Spirit*, where the recurring theme of his temptations was the opportunity to secure his future for himself (Matt. 4:1–11; Mark 1:12–13; Luke 4:1–13). Jesus refused. This Jesus is the one who not only lived but also died by the power of the Spirit. And by the power of the Spirit was this Jesus raised from death to life—radically new life *in the Spirit*. The pneumatological dimensions of Jesus's life cannot be overemphasized, for they are also the shape (*morphē*) of our own lives, which is also why it is appropriate to describe this characteristic as *terrifyingly* pneumatological. The path that Jesus walked so faithfully by the Spirit led inexorably to the cross, by way of Gethsemane. To live by the Spirit may well mean our political life is one where our grief wrings blood from our brow.[3]

The Christians who follow this Jesus as King know that they receive their future as a gift from God; they receive the future by the Spirit. Thus, they understand their political existence to be strikingly different from the future-securing struggle of the world around them. Winning and losing take on an entirely new cast, as do living and dying (Phil. 1:21). Pastors who seek to offer

---

3. See Luke 22:44 for this imagery.

political guidance will find the way of Jesus defined by the leading of the Spirit, and not by the lines of this or that political party's platform.

Conclusion and Prayer

At the end of all this, we may well be left questioning whether these characteristics are at all useful. After all, none of this tells me for whom I should vote, or even whether I should vote at all! This is true. If I could sit in my home in Boston in 2018 and give you detailed instructions for faithful, theopolitical action wherever and whenever you are, I would be ignoring the demand for the scandalous particularity that we have discussed here. I have suggested some ways this might take shape in the life of a Christian, or some possibilities for how a pastor might lead a congregation along these lines. Ultimately, however, the concrete ways in which we follow Jesus as King in our particular time and place is a matter of theological discernment by a church community seeking the leading of the Holy Spirit. As you go to engage in this scandalous, stubborn, terrifying way of life, pray this prayer with me for all those who have, do, and will follow Jesus in Caesar's presence:

> O God, you made us in your own image and redeemed us through Jesus your Son: Look with compassion on the whole human family; take away the arrogance and hatred that infect our hearts; break down the walls that separate us; unite us in bonds of love; and work through our struggle and confusion to accomplish your purposes on earth; that, in your good time, all nations may serve you in harmony around your heavenly throne; through Jesus Christ our Lord. Amen.[4]

---

4. "Prayers for the World, 'For the Human Family,'" *Book of Common Prayer*, 1979 edition, amended.

12 ✝ FOLLOWING JESUS IN PRAISE: THE SLAIN LAMB ON THE THRONE

Ryan L. Hansen

ONE DOESN'T usually expect to witness an apocalypse[1] in a food court. But that is exactly what happened when a flash mob, dressed inconspicuously like holiday shoppers and mall employees, emerged from a crowd to sing Handel's "Hallelujah Chorus" from his oratorio *Messiah*.[2] It begins as a woman having a conversation on her cell phone pushes back from the table, stands up, and boldly sings the first notes of the hymn of praise. Next, a man in a gray hoodie answers with "hallelujahs" of his own. They are joined by others, including a man dressed as a custodian and holding a "Wet Floor" sign. Soon, nearly a hundred voices flood a space that was formerly dominated by the sounds of cash registers, the scrape of chairs, and the smell of curly fries. The surprise choir declares boldly and beautifully that line from the song culled from the book of Revelation: "The kingdom of the world has become the kingdom of our Lord and of his Messiah, and he will reign forever and ever" (11:15).[3] What had been a place of casual consumption, or a quick resting spot before getting back to the frenzy, was

---

1. The word "apocalypse" comes from the Greek *apokalypsis*, which means something is revealed or unveiled. The word did not originally carry today's connotations of disaster and destruction.

2. "Christmas Food Court Flash Mob, Hallelujah Chorus," Alphabet Photography Inc (November 18, 2010), https://www.youtube.com/watch?v=SXh7JR9oKVE&feature =youtu.be.

3. All Scripture references in this chapter are NRSV, unless otherwise indicated.

suddenly transformed. You can see it in the faces of those unsuspecting witnesses of this act of bearing witness to Christ and his kingdom. The public declaration of praise to the King of kings and Lord of lords was a window into another reality—one they hardly expected to encounter in this place.

It might surprise more than a few people that these famous lines from Handel's *Messiah* come from Revelation. Many readers think of Revelation as a scary and exotic book, but many of the church's most beloved hymns and worship songs are drawn from the words and rich imagery found in Revelation. Revelation is saturated with scenes and songs of worship. To a large degree, worship—rather than scenes of disaster and judgment—drives the action of the Apocalypse of John.[4] The church's worship is also filled with language from the book of Revelation in its liturgy and hymns. In addition to the "Hallelujah Chorus," cherished hymns like "Holy, Holy, Holy! Lord God Almighty," "All Hail the Power of Jesus' Name," and "Crown Him with Many Crowns," as well as more recent choruses like "We Fall Down" and "Revelation Song" all employ language from Revelation.[5]

Just as the "Hallelujah Chorus" flash mob was a powerful symbol of the kingdom of God showing up in the here and now, declarations of praise in the book of Revelation were surprising and evocative proclamations that God's kingdom was coming to earth in dramatic and transformative ways. Worship functions in the Apocalypse of John to make not just theological claims but also political ones. Praise is always declaring someone to be the true Lord of this world. Praise always has to do with power. In Revelation, praise is directed toward a surprising object of power and authority: a slain Lamb occupies the throne at the center of all creation (5:6). Revelation's scenes of praise re-tune our conceptions of what it means to follow Jesus as King because he is a very different kind of king ruling a very different kind of kingdom.

---

4. Throughout this chapter, the last book of the Christian Bible will be referred to interchangeably as Revelation, the Apocalypse, or the Apocalypse of John, which are all traditionally accepted titles, especially since "Revelation" and "Apocalypse" should be taken as synonymous (see footnote 1).

5. These examples and others are noted by Michael J. Gorman in *Reading Revelation Responsibly: Uncivil Worship and Witness: Following the Lamb into the New Creation* (Eugene, OR: Cascade Books, 2011), 112–14.

Unveiling Worship

We often hear the phrase, or see it written on home décor: "When God closes a door, he opens a window." In the book of Revelation, however, God does not close doors; God opens them (3:8; 4:1; 21:25). Since worship is such an expansive topic in the Apocalypse, the image of the open door in Revelation 3:7–5:14 provides a helpful microcosm of what praise means in the book. In these three chapters we see the letters to two of the local churches to whom John addresses the book. Then we see the beginning of his heavenly vision in which he sees God and the Lamb on the throne, surrounded by a rightly ordered creation singing endless praise to them both. These three chapters provide a handy summary of what Revelation has to say about following Jesus in praise.

In Revelation 3, Christ addresses—through John's letter—two local congregations in Asia Minor: Philadelphia and Laodicea. These two congregations could not be more different. The church at Philadelphia is praised by Christ as faithful in their testimony and endurance, even though they "have but little power" (3:8). Perhaps their faithful witness through worship has cost them social status and cultural comfort. Nonetheless, Christ opens a door for them. Christ identifies himself as the one "who opens and no one will shut, who shuts and no one opens" (v. 7) and declares that he has placed before them "an open door" (v. 8).

Laodicea's Christians, on the other hand, see themselves as lacking nothing, wealthy and prosperous; they are utterly self-sufficient. Christ sees through this façade, calling them "wretched, pitiable, poor, blind, and naked" (v. 17). They have not kept true to their testimony to Christ, nor have they forsaken him completely. They are "lukewarm" Christians (v. 16), confessing Christ when it is convenient and leaving his name off their lips when it is not. Here the image is not of an open door but a closed one. Christ is outside, knocking, wishing to come in to share the Eucharistic feast with his church. Revelation 3:20 expresses his message to the closed-off Laodiceans: "If you hear my voice and open the door, I will come in to you and eat with you, and you with me." The contrast is clear: the Philadelphians have been faithful in their worship and stand before an open door, whereas the Laodiceans have neglected worship and have Christ knocking on their closed door.

The very next thing John sees is an open door in heaven (4:1), and when he peers inside he sees God on the throne, surrounded by four living creatures and twenty-four elders engaged in endless worship and praise of the one who created all things. The throne is the symbol of authority and governance signifying God's rule over all creation. Praise is the appropriate response to the one who has made all things and rules all things well. When the hymns of worship start, the elders cast down their crowns, showing that all authority in creation is subsumed under divine lordship (cf. Rev. 17:14). This also shows that praise and politics have more to do with each other than might seem at first to be the case.[6]

The door imagery suggests that more is going on in worship than a mere coming together to sing songs to God. In worship, God opens a door into heaven and reveals that the church's praise is a participation in what is happening continuously in heaven. Upon entering this door, the church finds itself ordered around the throne, along with all of creation. Praise brings the world before the throne of God and offers it as a gift while simultaneously bringing the lordship of Christ to bear in the world.[7] In worship, God opens a door so that the heavenly reality might spill down into the congregation and the world in which the congregation lives. Such is the importance of the public nature of the praise of the church: the church that worships is making a declaration about the truth of reality that may not always seem obvious to those not participating in praise.

A Tale of Two Salvations

After witnessing the worship service around the throne, John's gaze is directed toward a scroll in the right hand of the one on the throne. The scroll represents God's redemptive intentions for all of history, and may indeed contain the action that unfurls throughout the rest of Revelation. The scroll is sealed, and only one being is worthy to open the scroll: the conquering Lion of Judah. But when John turns to look at the ferocious Lion, he sees instead a slain Lamb, standing "in the midst of the throne" (5:6,

---

6. Indeed, the things ascribed to the one on the throne could hardly be described as apolitical: almighty, glory, honor, power (Rev. 4:8, 11; cf. 11:17).

7. For this aspect of the purpose of worship, see Alexander Schmemann, *For the Life of the World: Sacraments and Orthodoxy* (Crestwood, NY: St. Vladimir's Seminary Press, 1973), 11–22.

author's translation). The imagery here is hard to picture and works better on the symbolic, rather than literal, level.

First we have—to John's surprise and ours—the vision of a lamb rather than a lion. Both images are meant to inform each other. The Lion is not a violent conqueror or lurking predator, wreaking violence upon his prey; he is, rather, a slain-yet-living victim. The Lamb, in turn, viewed as an overlay of the Lion, may seem gentle and meek but holds the tremendous power to enact God's dramatic redemptive purposes for all of creation.

Second, the Lamb is standing *in the middle* of the throne. The Lamb is not standing *near* the throne or *between* the throne and the surrounding figures but right in the middle of it.[8] The implication is that the Lamb deserves the same worship as the one seated on the throne. But there is more than that going on as well. It is almost as if the Lamb is intertwined *with* the throne. Again, working on the symbolic level, as Revelation does, this image may be suggesting that the Lamb is intrinsic to the way God governs the world. The throne is the symbol of authority and rule, and the Lamb is the unexpectedly central part of that authority and rule.[9] This status is affirmed by the worship given to the Lamb and the one on the throne together, designating the Lamb as worthy of "power and wealth and wisdom and might" (5:12). The Lamb who gave his life on the cross is the way God governs the world.

In the enthronement and worship of the slain Lamb, the explosive power of praise begins to come into focus. In the first-century context of the book of Revelation, worship was not a category that belonged to Christians alone. In the Roman imperial and ancient Mediterranean world, everyone was a worshiper: the question was not whether you worshiped but, rather, whom you worshiped. The early Christians did not own the copyright on worship and praise; these were thoroughly Roman imperial concepts. Politi-

---

8. Some translations seek to avoid confusion by positioning the Lamb somewhere next to the throne.

9. Richard Bauckham explains, "When the slaughtered Lamb is seen 'in the midst of the divine throne in heaven' (5:6; cf. 7:17), the meaning is that Christ's sacrificial death *belongs to the way God rules the world." The Theology of the Book of Revelation* (Cambridge: Cambridge University Press, 1993), 64.

cal power and worship were not separate topics in this world, and they are likewise held together in the New Testament.[10]

In the Roman imperial context, worship was given over to a divinized Caesar and the Roman gods, who were praised for holding the world together. The worship of imperial Rome envisioned Rome at the center of all things and keeping everything in its right place through the subjection and domination of the rest of the world. Revelation depicts this worship of Caesar's military might in the song of those who worship the beast: "Who is like the beast, and who can fight against it?" (13:4). Caesar's conquest was said to make everything new and bring peace to the entire world. He was called "Savior" and "Lord" before Jesus was born, and the New Testament borrows the word "gospel" from reports of Roman military victories. The governor of the province of Asia Minor (the setting of John's seven churches), declared:

> (It is hard to tell) whether the birthday of the most divine Caesar is a matter of greater pleasure or benefit. We could justly hold it to be the beginning of all things, and he has restored . . . every form that had become imperfect and fallen into misfortune; and he has given a different aspect to the whole world, which blithely would have embraced its own destruction if Caesar had not been born for the common benefit of all. Therefore people would be right to consider this to have been the beginning of the life of breath for them.[11]

Carved on coins and statues and in the sacrificial temples that dominated the first-century urban landscape, this refrain of praise was repeated.[12] This

---

10. A prime example of this is Luke's Christmas narrative in Luke 1–2. See also James Chukwuma Okoye, "Power and Worship: Revelation in African Perspective" in *From Every People and Nation: The Book of Revelation in Intercultural Perspective*, ed. David Rhoads (Minneapolis: Fortress Press, 2005), 110–26. Chukwuma says, "Behind the activity of worship is the question of power: 'Who indeed is in charge of this world?' . . . True worship of God is always a threat to imperialists and rulers who would wield absolute and self-serving power" (124).

11. Quoted in S. R. F. Price, *Rituals and Power: The Roman Imperial Cult in Asia Minor* (Cambridge: Cambridge University Press, 1984), 55.

12. For good examples of this Roman imperial gospel, see the Judaea Capta coin, the Arch of Titus, the Ara Pacis altar, and the Prima Porta Augustus statue. In these images, Rome is envisioned as the center of the world while the conquered peoples of the world bow in submission to Caesar and the Roman gods. See also Paul F. Zanker, *The Power of Images in the Age of Augustus*, trans. Alan Shapiro (Ann Arbor: University of Michigan

---

kind of language and imagery was not mere flattery. Instead, it represents a confession of what the Roman Empire—its politicians and its people—believed to be the deepest truth about the world: Caesar governed the world and brought peace by dominating the nations through violence, making slaves of many peoples while glorifying the might of the empire (see Rev. 17:15; 18:13).[13]

The worship of the slain Lamb on the throne tells an altogether different story. The way God governs the world is not through domination and violence but, rather, through sacrificial love. The Lamb is not the last in a long line of violent and powerful conqueror-kings. Instead, God is present on earth "as the Lamb who conquers by suffering. Christ's suffering witness and sacrificial death are . . . the key event in God's conquest of evil and establishment of his kingdom on earth."[14] The way of imperialism and domination is an old song, playing on repeat through the ages as empires rise and fall. The hymn of praise to Christ is "a new song" proclaiming that the way God unifies all nations is not through conquest but by freeing them through the blood of the Lamb and making them participants in God's worshiping kingdom (1:5–6; 5:9–10).[15]

In this scene of worship, a tale of two salvations begins to emerge. Which kind of salvation have John's readers received, and who has accomplished it for them? Caesar or the Lamb—who is the true savior? To that

---

Press, 1988); Steven J. Friesen, *Imperial Cults and the Apocalypse of John: Reading Revelation in the Ruins* (Oxford: Oxford University Press, 2001).

13. Craig R. Koester states, "When human beings 'conquer,' they do so by inflicting death and damage on their adversaries. In John's time, the Roman armies had extended the borders of the empire through such conquest, capturing people of many tribes, languages, and nations. Captives in war typically became slaves, who were relegated to the lowest stratum of society . . . As further visions unfold, readers learn that many derive their wealth not from God—to whom all power and riches belong—but from 'Babylon,' where the beast and not the Lamb is honored, and where human beings are sold rather than freed." *Revelation and the End of All Things* (Grand Rapids: Eerdmans, 2001), 79–80). For an insightful interpretation of Revelation and the experiences of slavery in the Greco-Roman world and the American South, see Clarice J. Martin, "Polishing the Unclouded Mirror: A Womanist Reading of Revelation 18:13" in *From Every People and Nation*, 82–109.

14. Bauckham, *The Theology of the Book of Revelation*, 64.

15. For a convincing case about the all-encompassing scope of the Lamb's victory, see Bauckham, *The Theology of the Book of Revelation*, 66, where the twenty-eight occurrences of "Lamb" are said to correspond to the seven occurrences of every "nation, people, tongue, and language" (7 x 4 = 28).

one, praise is due. This presents a pressurized choice between whose songs of praise the congregants will sing. In Revelation, praise is not just coming together to sing pleasant songs to God; rather, worship of the Lamb is a pledge of allegiance to an entirely different kind of King and kingdom.[16] Caesar, who fancies himself the savior of the world, doesn't like his authority to be called into question (modern-day Caesars don't take too kindly to this either). Nor is John naïve about what he is calling his churches to do. Their witness to Christ in a Caesar-dominated world was likely challenging and painful.[17] If most of your neighbors believe their salvation comes from Caesar but you believe it is from Christ, they will notice when you do not praise Caesar for the good things they believe have come from his hand.[18]

Although all appearances were to the contrary for John's audience—Rome was the mightiest civilization in their world, and the slain Lamb himself had fallen under Caesar's dominating hand—through the open door of worship God revealed the truth of the way things are in heaven already and how they will be when the kingdom comes in its fullness (11:15). This is why the church in Philadelphia, though they "have but little power," has an open door set before them that no one can close (3:8). This is the reason for Jesus's persistent knocking on the door to the Laodicean gathering, so that he might come in and share his own Supper with them.[19] Through the open door of worship, the kingdom comes on earth as it is in heaven, even if it is not yet here in its fullness. This view through the door

---

16. No one was found worthy to open the sealed scroll in God's right hand—only the Lamb. No other way of ruling the world conforms perfectly to God's intent for creation—only the Lamb's way.

17. Bauckham puts it plainly: "Therefore the alternative becomes an utterly stark one: worship the beast or face martyrdom. The portrayal of the situation such that no one can escape this choice in this stark form embodies John's prophetic insight into the issue between church and empire: that there can be no compromise between the truth of God and the idolatrous lie of the beast." *The Theology of the Book of Revelation*, 93.

18. For more on the social cost of witness to Christ in John's context, see my discussion of this in Ryan L. Hansen, *Silence and Praise: Rhetorical Cosmology and Political Theology in the Book of Revelation* (Minneapolis: Fortress Press, 2014), 60–67. The refusal to worship Caesar was not merely a religious matter but had political, social, and economic implications and consequences.

19. Interestingly, Jesus also promises the Laodiceans that if they conquer they will be able to share Jesus's throne, just as Jesus conquered and shared the throne with the Father (Rev. 3:21). This is more evidence that, for the Apocalypse, worship and politics are inextricably linked.

of the way things are enables the church to bear witness to that reality in the world where things look contrary to that reality.

Songs of Endings and Beginnings

In the Church of the Nazarene, people are fond of talking about the radical optimism of grace—which is the idea that no person or situation is too far gone to be touched and transformed in significant ways by the boundless love and grace of God. John's Apocalypse may help us add to that vocabulary in a useful way. In the scenes of heavenly worship and earthly witness in Revelation, we see what I call the radical optimism of praise. When one reads through the hymns of Revelation, one cannot help but notice how powerful is their conviction that the kingdom of the Lamb is coming to every nation and people, every corner of God's creation. Praise, in the key of Revelation, is a bold declaration in a local time and place that the work of the slain Lamb will one day radically transform that place and, indeed, that the transformation is happening even now.

Praise is optimistic because it sings of endings and beginnings. It sings of the end of the misrule of Caesar (and all his imitators throughout history). When John sees an uncountable multitude in heaven singing, "Salvation belongs to our God who is seated on the throne, and to the Lamb!" (7:10), he is witnessing a declaration of regime change. Another hymn boldly declares, "The kingdom of the world has become the kingdom of our Lord and of his Messiah, and he will reign forever and ever" (11:15). Later, a mighty angel sings victoriously, "Fallen, fallen is Babylon the great!" (18:2).[20] The songs of praise that give all authority and glory and saving power to God and the Lamb mean that none of it goes to Caesar or Rome. The Lamb's rule means Caesar's rule and ways are at an end. The reign of terror, enslavement, and exploitation that many living within the boundaries of the empire face daily has its days numbered, and the violence

---

20. Babylon as a metaphor for Rome represents Christian opposition to Rome by conjuring up visions of Israel's old oppressor—the empire that sent Judah into exile and destroyed their First Temple (587 BCE). By the first century CE, Rome was not only the most powerful empire that had oppressed God's people but was also the imperial force that destroyed the Second Temple. The parallels would be obvious to anyone who knew Israel's history but would likely be obscure to the Romans.

and domination that characterize that rule will be excluded from the coming kingdom (7:16–17; 21:4, 27).[21]

Knowing that this rule has met its end, citizens of the Lamb's kingdom
are freed to live life differently. But this loss of Caesar's kingdom does not
come without cost for those followers of the Lamb who are still drawn to
the comforts of Caesar's kingdom. John's churches include plenty whose
livelihoods depend on them being on good terms with the worship of imperial power (e.g., merchants, sailors, and local artisans and business owners;
see 18:1–24).[22] The call to follow the Lamb is always a call to take up one's
cross (Mark 8:34), and it means stepping out of one world (Caesar's) and
into another (God's new creation). Revelation's consistent message is that
Caesar's world must come to an end because of the way it misuses and
mishandles God's good creation.[23]

Where Caesar's kingdom misconstrues and misuses, the Lamb's reign
heals (Rev. 7:15–17; 21:3–7; 22:1–2). Praise sings of the end of Caesar's reign
in order to sing even more loudly of the beginning of the Lamb's reign.
And the Lamb's reign brings new possibility and potential to everything,
even the things where no potential existed. The one on the throne declares,
"See, I am making all things new" (21:5). It is important to remember that
the new creation is not a replacement creation but a renewed creation. The
new creation is the world that has finally, fully come under the lordship of
Christ the King. As such, it is a place wholly devoted to worshiping God

---

21. Barbara R. Rossing says, "Everything about the old order of fear and domination, of
imperial violence and injustice, must be left behind." *The Rapture Exposed: The Message of
Hope in the Book of Revelation* (New York: Basic Books, 2004), 151.

22. Brian K. Blount argues in his commentary: "In a classic 'Don't ask, don't tell' (that
I am a Christian) kind of environment, John was essentially ordering his Christians to be
about the business of telling on themselves, with full knowledge of the kind of repercus-
sions that such telling would bring." *Revelation: A Commentary* (Louisville: Westminster
John Knox Press, 2009), 118.

23. Dale C. Allison, Jr., says, "Proclaiming a near end . . . bring[s] to dramatic and
needed expression the divine discontent with . . . a world bad enough that it needs to be
improved out of existence." *The Historical Christ and the Theological Jesus* (Grand Rapids:
Eerdmans, 2009), 98.

and the Lamb.[24] Those who follow the Lamb in praise are given "eyes to see the whole world with a kind of sacramental vision."[25]

Those who praise the Lamb have seen through the door of worship into God's ultimate purpose for all creation. Their imaginations have been formed by the vision of all creation gathered in praise around the throne of God and the Lamb. They have seen what it looks like when everything is in its right place (5:11–14), and are therefore commissioned to bear witness to the renewal that is on its way for every nook and cranny of this world and every person who inhabits it.[26] Those who worship the Lamb have been claimed by and belong to the one who makes all things new—they are citizens of the New Jerusalem. Their worship fills the present with possibility, declaring an end to fears and frustrated hopes and making the audacious claim that life and newness are available no matter how difficult things appear.[27] If a slain Lamb can stand victorious on the throne at the center of the universe, the new creational possibilities are limitless for those with eyes to see and ears to hear.[28] Worship is the invitation to this kind of sanctified imagination (22:17).

---

24. Worship of the Lamb is the way of life in the New Jerusalem; therefore, there is no need for a temple (Rev. 21:22). Every facet of life will be hallowed, consecrated, set apart for God's glory and holy purpose. See Koester, *Revelation and the End of All Things*, 197–98.

25. Rossing, *The Rapture Exposed*, 161.

26. "The act of worship rehearses in the present the end that lies ahead." Eugene H. Peterson, *Reversed Thunder: The Revelation of John and the Praying Imagination* (San Francisco: Harper & Row, 1988).

27. Rossing makes this analogy: "As they come back from behind the apocalyptic veil, the Christians of Ephesus now see their own city more dearly, glimpsed in a new and deeper way. Like Scrooge waking up from his visions or Dorothy waking up in Kansas, everything is different now because of their life-changing apocalyptic journey." *The Rapture Exposed*, 163.

28. "I like to ask people to . . . re-phrase the vision of New Jerusalem in terms of their own city's renewal, like [Martin Luther] King's vision of the New Philadelphia, the New Los Angeles: 'I saw the holy city, God's New (*Name of Your Town*) coming down out of heaven . . .' What would your 'new' city look like? This is an exercise in 'borrowing the eyes of God,' as the German theologian Dorothee Soelle describes our mystical sight. We see our world as God sees it. This is what happens in Revelation's New Jerusalem vision." Rossing, *The Rapture Exposed*, 166.

Following the slaughtered Lamb fills the everyday with the radical optimism of praise.[29] In worship, one is freed to imagine renewed life in every place, for every person one encounters. New possibilities emerge everywhere. One is free to ask and imagine how the Lamb's victory might inform the ways we consume goods and spend money, what symbols of status define our lives, how we relate to our neighbors, and how we might share meals together with "glad and generous hearts" (Acts 2:46)—even, perhaps, in the food court of a shopping mall.

---

29. The New Testament witness is consistent that Christian patterns of thinking and acting in their present day are shaped to a large extent by the defining reality of the day of the Lord. Thus, their everyday is infused with the power and possibility of the fulfillment of all of God's promises in Christ.

✝ CONCLUSION

Timothy R. Gaines

THROUGH parched lips and strained lungs, a bleeding man on the verge of his death uttered these words: "It is finished" (John 19:30). It is a fitting statement, perhaps, for one so near the end of his life. Save these few utterances, his life is all but over—finished—in the way a book comes to an end when the last page is turned.

Enfolded into the meaning of the single word that conveys "it is finished," though, is a more nuanced understanding of what it means to *be* finished. The word John has chosen to communicate Jesus's last message from the cross is one that signals not simply that something has come to an end but that something has reached its fulfillment. We could say that his choice of this word implies that being "finished" does not close off the future, as death so often does, but opens a new kind of future altogether.

In what sense, then, was Jesus finished as he hung his head and died? In all likelihood, there were some who witnessed his death and bore the anguish of watching him be finished off by the agents of a powerful military who nailed his body to that execution device. Others, perhaps, looked on with a sense of satisfaction, exhaling a sigh of relief and trusting that a season of unrest, brought about by a rebellious fomenter who refused to get in line, was finally finished. If those people had written the account, I suspect they would have chosen a different word to describe what they were witnessing. They saw an end. John, however, saw a fulfillment, opening a new future.

"*Tetelestai*," John inscribes in Greek in his account of Jesus's death. It is not wrong of us to translate this word as the familiar phrase "It is finished." Yet we cannot allow the notion of being finished to include a closing off of the future. This word—which grows from a common root as others that signal a sense of completion, consummation, or fulfillment—is instilled with potential in this context, like the weed that presses through a crack in the concrete. When you have paved over a wild plot of land, bringing it under your control and taming its ability to bring forth its unwieldy growth, only to find a bit of green pressing its way up, disrupting your best efforts, you have touched on this statement's implications. Jesus's death on the cross could be seen as the silencing of a disorderly prophet. His crucifixion could signal the closing off of the kind of mediation an out-of-line priest may offer. The crown of thorns upon his head and the inscription upon his cross were certainly meant to gesture to the triumph over a pretender king. He was finished.

But what if his last words from the cross carry the connotation of fulfillment? What if his death was not shutting him down but opening a new future to all who would come after him? What if his broken body itself is not only the prophetic call to God's people to live faithfully to God but is also the very fulfillment of a life lived in utter faithfulness? What might it mean if his work as priest, echoing his priestly ancestors, continued to sprinkle blood over the people—but that the blood he pours over them is his own? What do we do with a king who takes the very symbols meant to mock his failure and explodes their meaning by making them the hallmarks of true kingship? In short, we follow him.

Our following, however, is not only a foolish act of defiance. To be sure, it takes on the distinct flavor of prophetic defiance, and it depends upon a kind of life that appears foolish to those who see the cross as having finished off Jesus (1 Cor. 1:18). But, in the fulfilling work that Jesus does as prophet, priest, and king, he opens a new future to us, and we follow him into that future. We act, think, live, and work prophetically, calling over and over again to God's people to remember who and whose they are, and to live a life worthy of the good news that Jesus has opened this future to us (Phil. 1:27).

We allow Jesus to mediate a God to us who has been revealed to be the kind of God who acts to redeem us at God's own expense. We order our lives under his kingship, knowing that following a king whose crown is made of thorns will not likely result in the kind of political glory and economic greatness that is pursued by the very empire that nailed him to a cross. Jesus opens to us a future in which the prophetic call to faithfulness has been filled out by his complete faithfulness. He opens to us a future in which the mediating work of a priest has been fulfilled in his ability to be both God and human in one priest. He initiates a reality in which kingship is emptied of its need to lift up the king at the expense of the people. From the cross, lifted up for all to see, Jesus becomes the shocking, world-turning fulfillment of a prophet, a priest, and a king. It is *finished*.

The finished/fulfilled work of Prophet, Priest, and King Jesus opens to us a new reality. It invites us to follow him into that reality. Perhaps that is why John does not seem to want to be all that prescriptive with his accounts of Jesus's resurrection. In the concluding chapters of his Gospel, there is an account of the empty tomb (20:4–10); Jesus's appearance to Mary (20:14–18); and several instances in which Jesus comes to be with his disciples (20:19–29; 21:9–19). We also have a story about Jesus directing them toward a plentiful catch of fish, and a powerful conversation between Jesus and Peter in which Jesus graciously opens a way for Peter to remain faithful (21:1–19). Among these resurrection accounts, John indicates that "Jesus performed many other signs in the presence of his disciples, which are not recorded in this book" and "Jesus did many other things as well" (20:30; 21:25). The absence of the details and full resolution can be frustrating. Why would John leave things out? Why not take this opportunity to further prove Jesus was resurrected or to offer specific instructions for Christian life? But perhaps John wishes to conclude his book the way I am attempting to conclude this one: by pointing to a new future that has been opened up and inviting others to follow Jesus into it.

In this sense, then, this book cannot conclude as if it is finished when you turn the last page. Rather, it concludes—it is finished—in John's sense of the word. It opens up a new future and invites us to step into it. In a few moments, you will turn the last page of this book and finish reading. It will be finished. In one sense, you may finish this book, close it, and it will remain a closed reality of the past. But our hope in writing this kind of book is that it also opens a new kind of future to you when the last page is turned and the book returns to the shelf. To borrow John's words, "But these are written that you may believe that Jesus is the Messiah, the Son of God, and that by believing you may have life in his name" (John 20:31). That new kind of future—the life in his name—is opened to us by the way Jesus finished the work of a prophet, a priest, and a king. And his finishing work now issues an invitation to us. Will you follow him into the future he has opened?

✝ ABOUT THE AUTHORS

Dick O. Eugenio, PhD, serves in the Philippines as associate professor of theology at Asia-Pacific Nazarene Theological Seminary. He also pastors Taytay First Church of the Nazarene. He is married to Mary Ann, and together they are blessed with two children, Heloise and Jedidiah.

Timothy R. Gaines, PhD, serves as assistant professor of religion at Trevecca Nazarene University in Nashville, Tennessee. In addition to teaching theology and ethics, he serves as a staff pastor for university students and is a frequent speaker and preacher. He is married to Shawna, with whom he co-authored *A Seat at the Table: A Generation Re-imagining Its Place in the Church* and *Kings and Presidents: Politics and the Kingdom of God*.

Timothy Green, PhD, is the dean of the Millard Reed School of Theology and Christian Ministry at Trevecca Nazarene University and professor of Old Testament literature and theology. In addition to teaching and speaking around the world, he has also authored numerous articles and books, including a volume in the *New Beacon Bible Commentary* on Hosea, Joel, Amos, Obadiah, Jonah, and Micah and, most recently, *The God Plot: Living with Holy Imagination*.

Timothy L. P. Hahn, MA, MDiv, spends all of his time talking about the two things you're not supposed to mention in polite company: theology and politics. A graduate of Southern Nazarene University and Nazarene Theological Seminary, Tim has pastored in Kansas City and Philadelphia. He is married to Laura, and the two live in Boston, where he is currently a PhD student studying theology at Boston University.

Ryan L. Hansen, PhD, is an independent biblical scholar and an ordained elder in the Church of the Nazarene. He has served churches in Chicago and Nashville and has taught classes at Garrett-Evangelical Theological Seminary, Olivet Nazarene University, and Northwest Nazarene University. His most recent book is *Silence and Praise: Rhetorical Cosmology and Political Theology in the Book of Revelation*.

Diane Leclerc, PhD, graduated from Eastern Nazarene College, Nazarene Theological Seminary, and Drew University. She has published numerous articles and seven books, including *Discovering Christian Holiness*. In addition to being professor of historical theology at Northwest Nazarene University, she presently serves as pastor to university students at Nampa College Church of the Nazarene.

Kara Lyons-Pardue, PhD, is associate professor of New Testament at Point Loma Nazarene University. Kara loves reading and talking about the New Testament so much that she almost always lets her classes out late. Her favorite Gospel is Mark because of its enigmatic portrayal of Jesus, who is always on the move. She is the mother of two wonderful little girls and is married to Charlie, a fellow minister.

Stephanie Smith Matthews, MTS, is a PhD candidate in Hebrew Bible and ancient Israel at Vanderbilt University. She currently serves as a teaching extern in Old Testament at Columbia Theological Seminary in Decatur, Georgia. A licensed minister in the Church of the Nazarene, Stephanie strives to help others recognize the voice of God in the Old Testament.

Gift Mtukwa, MA, was born and raised in Harare, Zimbabwe, and currently lives in Nairobi, Kenya, where he teaches Bible and theology at Africa Nazarene University. He is an ordained minister with the Church of the Nazarene and serves as the lead pastor of University Church of the Nazarene. He is currently pursuing a PhD in biblical studies at the University of Manchester in England.

Amy Peeler, PhD, is associate professor of New Testament at Wheaton College and associate rector at St. Mark's Episcopal Church in Geneva, Illinois. Author of *"You Are My Son": The Family of God in the Epistle to the Hebrews*, she continues to research the theological language of family across the New Testament.

Mary K. Schmitt, MDiv, is a PhD candidate at Princeton Theological Seminary, serving as assistant professor of New Testament at Trevecca Nazarene University in Nashville, Tennessee. She is an ordained elder in the Church of the Nazarene. Her primary area of research is on conflict and peace in Paul's letter to the Romans.

David Young, MDiv, is a PhD candidate in New Testament studies at Boston University. Prior to pursing further studies, he was privileged to serve as pastor of Clinton First Church of the Nazarene in Clinton, Illinois, for six years. He continues to enjoy serving in ministry by teaching at Lowell First Church of the Nazarene and preaching in churches across New England. He and his wife have been gifted with three remarkable children.